To: Sara

Airmail and Chocolate Pie
Back to Boonetown

Bobby Evers

My Best, Bobby Evers

Copyright © 2024 Bobby Evers
Published by Berger Street Press
For more information : www.bobbyevers.com
All rights reserved. No part of this book may be used or reproduced in any form or by any means, electronic or mechanical or in performance, including photocopying, recording, or any information storage and retrieval system without express written permission from the author.

ISBN 978-1-7374175-7-6
First Edition
10 9 8 7 6 5 4 3 2 1

Editor: Wordsmith Collaborative, Nashville, TN
Cover Graphics: Meltmama Creative Studio
Original Cover Artwork: Bobby Evers . All rights reserved.

To the fabulous Harlettes

Acknowledgements

My thanks to Carolyn German of Wordsmith Collaborative for editing, advice, encouragement, and always being a great sounding board. I'm so glad you have been with me on this writing journey.

And always, my deepest appreciation to the friends and family who support, encourage, and offer expertise and assistance in my writing endeavors. I couldn't do it without you.

THE STORIES

Introduction	1
Dateline: Obsessed	3
High Maintenance	11
Truth in Advertising	21
I'm Not So Excited	27
Good Morning, Dolly	35
Airmail and Chocolate Pie	41
Dr. Karma	55
Paris 3.0	61
A Day at the Beach	75
Tour of Homes	81
The Green Café	89
Giving Care	97
Hair's the Thing	107
My Left Foot	115
What's the Point?	127
Boonetown Square	135
Speak Up	145
A Parade Passes By	153
Wardrobe Dysfunction	165
An Old Office, An Old Friend	173
'Twas an Evers Family Christmas	185
I'm Afraid	191
You Know	199

Introduction

Things change.

One day you think you are settled in for a while, with plans to write a new play. People occasionally asked me if a new book was in the works, and I'd say, "No, not anytime soon." I'd written a few stories that I liked, but I just wasn't feeling the desire to work on another book. I wanted to try something different.

At least that's what I was thinking.

Then, out of the blue, my nephew got a phone call, and picked up a bag someone found in an old shed: a seventy-year-old duffle bag of my dad's. You wouldn't think that would change any of my immediate plans, but it did.

Suddenly, I was reading letters. Lots of letters. Letters sent from my mom to my dad when he was in the military. And a story was forming in my head as quickly as I could digest the words on the pages.

Suddenly, I was writing stories I felt a strong emotional connection to, stories I wanted to publish. It felt very much as if I were getting a kick in the pants from my parents, urging me to keep writing.

They both died long before I wrote anything, so I

always wondered what they might think about my books. Would they be proud? Offended? Shocked?

That very unexpected discovery sent me on a writing journey, with renewed enthusiasm for the practice of storytelling. It fueled my desire to publish this book, and it re-connected me with my mom and dad in a new way.

So, yes, things do change. Sometimes in the most unexpected way. And then your mind changes, your focus changes and, suddenly, you have a new book to share.

It's a book I am proud to share. I hope you enjoy.

DATELINE: OBSESSED

If you have read anything of mine, then you know by now that I really, really love true crime television shows—especially *Dateline*. I used to only watch episodes on Thursday or Friday nights when they would originally air. Then I began recording them so I could see any shows I missed. After a while, *Dateline* began re-airing their older episodes on other channels, and I was certainly there for that too. I didn't care how many times I had seen these criminals brought to justice. I wanted to take part in their arrest time and time again.

I watched many *20/20* episodes, too. But I couldn't rely on them like *Dateline* because sometimes, if there was a big news event that week, *20/20* would slip in some current news coverage instead of their true crime stories. I suppose I should want to know all about the man that might become the next leader of my country but, just to be honest, I was much more interested in the pharmacist next door that was slowly poisoning his girlfriend. The latest presidential debates? Not so curious.

I was beginning to think I was the only person totally obsessed with these shows. I didn't talk about

Dateline: Obsessed

it much because I was kind of embarrassed to share with friends just how much time I was wasting on true crime. Then, when streaming took over the world and I got Hulu, it hit me that I must not be alone. I was home sick one day and got bored looking at their menu so I decided to do a search for true crime. I was astounded.

There are so many true crime series now that they are grouped by theme. The true crime documentary genre seems to have become a national obsession.

There have always been quite a few shows of the "unsolved" variety. One of the earliest was *Unsolved Mysteries*, and then we had *Cold Case Files*, *Cold Justice*, *Blood Runs Cold*, and any number of others.

But now they are getting even more specific. Now we have series like: *Hometown Homicide*, *Welcome to Murdertown*, *City Confidential*, and *Home Sweet Homicide*. Or you can watch episodes about murder between spouses. There are so many to choose from, like *Killer Affair*, *My Crazy Ex*, *Deadly Wives*, *Sleeping with Death*, *Married to Evil*, *Killer Brides*, and *Love, Honor, Betray*.

One true crime show I really get into is *Cold Justice*. The main investigator, Kelly Seigler is a total badass. She's a former prosecutor and uses her experience—as well as the expertise of a bevy of experts—to solve cold cases. Some of them are really old, like forty years or more. Nothing intimidates Kelly though, and she, amazingly, has a pretty good success rate. The only problem is they don't produce many episodes per season. So, I can't get nearly enough satisfaction from *Cold Justice*—even though I love it dearly.

I'm a little afraid though that with more and more advances in DNA, the cases might become less interesting over time. I know you can't solve a case with DNA alone, but once the DNA match is made, it's pretty much over. So sometimes *Dateline* really has to do a lot of stretching to fill a full two-hour episode. *Dateline* certainly is a master in the art of stretching, and I'm not talking about yoga. As much as I love them, sometimes they can really drag things out: a lot of the two-hour episodes really should be just one hour. But it's *Dateline* so I'll let that pass, since they are the gold standard of true crime.

I have to admit a lot of the newer shows are interesting. But I've caught a lot of them profiling cases that I've already seen on *Dateline*. And it's just hard to beat the way *Dateline*'s Keith Morrison can make his voice sound "spooky" or "eerie" when he is explaining the events leading up to a body being found out in the woods. Or the way he can act confused when interviewing an obviously guilty suspect. Sure, he can be a bit much, but when you are dealing with a murder, I think some voice affects are needed.

I've noticed other things too. For instance, Andrea Canning has been upping her fashion game in the last years. She's upped the height of her heels — they look like Louboutins — and her jeans have gotten a lot tighter. I've noticed that she has a lot of Van Cleef & Arpels jewelry now as well. I think she's trying to make up for the male hosts who obviously couldn't care less about their style — like Josh Mankiewicz. He might be my favorite though — I like his laidback style.

I've recently noticed that a lot of the new shows

are not using an on-air correspondent, and just let the witnesses introduce themselves. I guess that's ok, but it just doesn't seem to have that same feel as *Dateline*.

Certainly, though, the thing I find most fascinating is the lengths that some of the suspects will go to in order to get away with the crime. I remember one episode in particular where the suspect knew he had left DNA behind. So he obviously also knew that if he gave a DNA sample, he would be caught. On the other side of the coin, he knew that if he didn't offer to give a DNA sample, he would give himself away.

So he devised a rather ingenious plan.

As it turned out, the man was a doctor himself, and somehow he was able to insert a tiny tube full of someone else's blood into his own arm, at the inside of his elbow, where blood is normally drawn. How he got that tube in his arm without leaving bruises and a mark is still a big question, but he did. At the DNA test, he used his status as a doctor, to sort of direct the nurse who was drawing his blood. He held up his arm and pointed to this large vein in his arm that was actually the tube he had inserted. He kept his sleeve tight around his arm and only revealed the part of his arm where the tube was.

And it actually worked. They tested the imposter blood from the tube in his arm, which didn't match the criminal's sample. He evaded arrest for several years until the victim hired a private detective who covertly secured a sample of his DNA from his saliva and found that he was an exact match to the crime scene sample. He almost got away with it.

The most despicable character that was profiled on one of these shows was, without a doubt, the woman who killed both of her husbands for their insurance, and then tried to kill her own daughter — and frame the daughter for killing the two husbands. She thought she would end up scot-free. But, in the end, she gave herself away with a spelling error. (Actually, when I think about it, that will probably be what does me in too. Spelling has never been a strong point of mine.)

It went like this. The woman (I can't remember her name) had two daughters with her first husband, and he died of a mysterious illness. She immediately buried him and insisted on no autopsy. Then she was somehow able to quickly work through her grief and marry another unfortunate man a year or so later. This man also died of a mysterious illness, but this time the police were tipped-off by his family who strongly disliked his wife. The detectives began to suspect poisoning might be the cause of his death and questioned her about antifreeze. (If you watch any true crime at all, you know antifreeze is big in the spousal poisoning game.) Coincidentally, they had found some in her home.

Of course, she denied everything, and said she didn't know anything about "antifree." It is important to note that she called it antifree, not antifreeze. So the police, after talking to witnesses, began to suspect that she may have poisoned both husbands. This is where it really gets crazy. This woman was obviously a total narcissist and would do anything — I mean anything — to keep herself out of jail.

So, she devised an evil plan. As any good mother would, she asked her fifteen-year-old daughter to get drunk with her one night. (Mother of the year, she would not win.) The mother prepared a drink laced with alcohol and antifreeze. After the daughter drank the potion and went to sleep, the mom forged a suicide note that would free her from all responsibility. Or so she thought. It actually sealed her fate. I'm paraphrasing here, but the note went something like this:

"I am the daughter of (I-still-can't-remember-her-name) and I can no longer live with the guilt I am feeling, so I am killing myself with antifree. But first I have to confess to the other terrible things I have done. When I was eleven, I didn't like my father, so I poisoned him with antifree. My mother had nothing to do with it. And then when I was fifteen, I didn't like my mother's second husband either, so I poisoned him with antifree, too. My mother had nothing to do with this either. It was all me. I am a very bad daughter, so I am now poisoning myself, but before I die, I just want to make sure you know the truth, so that my innocent mother does not go to jail."

With one fell swoop the murdering mother thought she would win a get-out-of-jail-free card and receive the added bonus of more life insurance money.

But wait. It didn't work. The mother's genius plan failed. For one thing, she gave herself away with the misspelling of antifree. Secondly, she didn't put enough antifree in her daughter's drink. The daughter woke up, and denied killing anyone. The mother went to jail for murder and attempted murder.

But I'll give her credit: she stuck to her story to the end. That's one thing I've learned by watching *Dateline*. Stick to your story. You always get caught when you start changing up your story. These criminals always think they are smart enough to talk their way out of trouble. Many times, they might not have even been a suspect if they had just kept their mouth shut, but they can't help themselves. They think they are smarter than the detectives and start running their mouth. Big mistake.

So that's my number one take-away from *Dateline*. Ask for an attorney, and keep your mouth shut.

I know that might make you look more guilty, but since you are probably guilty anyway, don't dig the hole deeper. Don't you know they are recording every word you say? And you will get caught in your own lies. It amazes me how many people talk out loud to themselves after the detectives leave the interrogation room. Don't these people know about cameras? They are everywhere and you are being recorded. You are probably going to get caught with DNA evidence anyway, but just in case they don't have any, keep your big mouth shut.

There are so many other lessons I've learned on that show, too. Like if they can't find the murder weapon, look in the river, under the bridge, on the way home from the crime scene. The gun—often along with a bag of bloody clothes—will usually be found there.

Also, if there is a preacher involved in the episode, or if someone acting overly religious, talking about what a good Christian he is, he will turn out to be the killer—just bank on it. The more religious he acts, the more likely he has also already cleared-out the victim's bank account and slept with their wife.

Or, if your normally uninterested and unromantic husband suddenly wants to take you on a romantic hike in the mountains, don't, under any circumstances, go. You are about to be pushed off a cliff.

If your disgruntled business partner calls and says, "Let's meet at the office on Sunday," —when no one is there— "to have a confidential discussion about the future of the business," look out. You are undoubtedly going to end up dead, stored-away in an oil drum in the warehouse, while he runs off to the islands under an assumed name using your company stock.

If your unhappy, complaining, and cheating wife is suddenly very attentive to you and starts bringing you your "favorite drink" every evening when you get home for work, don't drink it! It's an antifreeze-laced screw-driver. You are probably already half-full of poison and don't even know it.

And certainly anytime you find yourself in an unhappy marriage, with lots of arguments, calls to the police, and verbal threats, and your spouse suddenly starts being really nice—watch out. If he invites you to "start fresh with a romantic picnic, or a second honeymoon," decline. Do. Not. Go. You won't come back alive.

Trust me, I've done the research through many hours of true crime viewing.

So, thank you, *Dateline*. You have provided me with shareable wisdom and so many hours of entertainment. You have also upped my levels of paranoia. Your in-depth coverage of violent crime has encouraged me to be suspicious of my neighbor, to never trust my spouse, and to stay far away from the edge of a cliff. I'll never trust anyone again… and I'll see you next Friday night.

HIGH MAINTENANCE

Going to the doctor has changed. The days of having one doctor that handles most everything are over and done. I'm not sure if things are better now or not, but you will definitely put a lot more miles on your car if you get sick. These days, any illness involves at least one referral to a specialist —maybe more.

I like to think I am pretty healthy, but I still have more doctors than I can count. The trips to the specialists began a couple of decades ago. I was having a lot of allergy problems so, of course, I ended up at an ENT for about ten years' worth of allergy shots.

Around that same time, I started having some prostate issues, so I was referred to a urologist. After that, some arthritis symptoms got me an appointment with a rheumatologist. Then I turned fifty and it was time for a colonoscopy, so I was referred to a colorectal doctor.

I have to add a little sidebar here. Of all the specialists I have been to, the colorectal doctor had the best outlook and the most upbeat personality. Now here is a man who literally spends all day, every day, poking around in people's butts, and he was all smiles. I know I have said it before, but it is worth repeating: Attitude is everything.

A year or so ago, at my six-month visit for bloodwork, I casually mentioned to my regular doctor that my brother had recently died of a heart attack. The next thing I knew, I was at a cardiologist's having a stress test.

Then, within a couple months of turning sixty, I suddenly started seeing these odd strings in my vision, so I was immediately referred to a retina specialist and, as luck would have it, I did have a torn retina, which he repaired.

Right after the torn retina, I casually bit down on something and broke a filling in a tooth. Thus began a month-long saga that ended up with a referral to an endodontist for a root canal.

And of course, I can't forget my bout with plantar fasciitis, but that's another story.

Thank goodness all these doctors are available to take care of me. But it does make me think about something my dad used to say, and I really have to agree with him on this. He would always give his doctor friends a really hard time about how they could only treat one thing on a human being—like your heart, or your feet—but a veterinarian could treat everything on an animal. And the vet could also treat an untold number of different types of animals. Dad thought this made human doctors look like a one-trick pony, and he would often tell them so.

We took our dogs to the same vet for a heart condition, a bad cut, a sore tooth, or a limp. My aunt took her cats to that same vet for all their cat

High Maintenance

problems from infections to a claw trim. This same vet would extract teeth, detect heart murmurs, remove tumors and so on. And this was just in dogs and cats. He would also treat your horse for a bad case of diarrhea, and figure out why your iguana suddenly stopped eating.

This vet would even attempt to discover if your pet boa constrictor was acting weird because of a back sprain, or maybe a bad urinary tract infection. (I have no idea if a boa constrictor even has a urinary tract, but I bet my vet would know. He knows everything.)

What's even more amazing is that vets have to figure it all out without any help from the patient. They can't talk. So vets are also mind-readers. It's really impressive.

Now I'm still wondering if snakes have a urinary tract. Come to think of it, I've never seen a snake taking a sip of water—surely, they do. You would think they would need some water to wash down those wild boars, or large rodents, or something equally unbelievable that you see them swallowing on National Geographic specials. I've always wondered how long it takes to digest something that size, eaten whole. I get a bad case of reflux if I eat a heavy meal after 8 p.m. And by heavy meal I mean something like pasta. Not a fully grown, fur-covered animal. I can't imagine the indigestion. So, it would seem like snakes must have a urinary tract.

Suddenly I am wondering if a snake does number one, or number two, or both, or a combination. And where exactly might it come out?

A vet would know.

There may even be vets that specialize in animal urology, and animal heart disease and so on. But in my small hometown, we have no such animal specialists. Just a couple of all-purpose, all-animal vets, which I still think must be some of the smartest people on the planet.

The family doctor of my childhood was more like a veterinarian in the respect that he treated us for everything. His office was only a few blocks from our home and right across from the general hospital.

I do remember him as being very confident, and a straight-shooter. He delivered me, my brother, and my sister, and was our doctor until he retired about the time I went to college.

He weighed a good ninety-five pounds, smoked, and drank a good bit. Luckily for him, he never gained weight, even with his bad habits. He would advise my parents to lose weight and this irritated my mom and dad greatly since they knew he did nothing —like eat healthy or exercise—to retain his super-low weight.

His office was a memorable one. It was shockingly well-designed and totally out of place in Boonetown. The building was long and low, with kind of a Frank Lloyd Wright influence. It had some stacked-stone accents by the entry doors and at a few other spots. The reception desk was framed with stone as well. There was one nurse there that answered the phone, assisted him with various in-patient surgeries, and also did the bookkeeping. Come to think of it, she was kind of amazing too: multifaceted, like a vet, but with different talents.

The waiting room had very distinctive black,

wrought-iron, mid-century-styled furniture with burnt-red, olive-green, and gold cushions. It was obvious that someone with very good taste had put it all together. Back then I didn't even know about interior designers, but I'd say he had one, as well as an architect.

I think you can tell a lot about a doctor by the way his waiting room looks. I'm not saying that it necessarily indicates the quality of care you will be receiving, but it does say something about how they feel about the image they are presenting, and the type of practice they have.

Of course, I try my best not to let the waiting room décor influence my opinion of the person, because you never know who might have decorated the office. The inhabitant may have had little to no influence on the décor.

Still, it's hard not to judge.

At the endodontist, the waiting room was a literal time-capsule. It was filled with vintage '80s furniture, upholstered in brightly hued Herculon — that wondrous fabric that is totally indestructible. And, true to form, it was in perfect condition. This was, without a doubt, the largest collection of nicotine-stain-free Herculon I'd ever seen.

From this waiting room I assumed — correctly — that the doctor would be older and probably nearing retirement. The lobby, even if vintage, was spotless, so I was not worried about cleanliness or staph infections. I also assumed — correctly — that the exam rooms would be spotless, with painfully out-of-date décor.

When I got into the dental chair, I found the

doctor to be extremely nice. But as he was thoroughly explaining the procedure, I was again puzzled by the décor. I could not help but notice — staring me in the face — a circa-1985 silk ficus tree. It wasn't just any fake tree though, this one had stuffed animals hanging around amongst the leaves. I suppose they were there to make you feel more relaxed. I thought that was what the gas was for, but maybe I was wrong. There was even a stuffed ball-of-sunshine with a happy face, just hanging on a branch to lift your spirits.

During his little talk, he told me that there were four canals in each tooth going down each of the four prongs of the root. He said he would have to drill into the tooth to find and clear-out each canal. He mentioned it could be difficult to find every canal. But I was thinking, since the overall size of a tooth is not much bigger than the eraser-end of a pencil, how hard could it be?

After a good bit of drilling, he said he had found two of the canals. So I'm thinking this is going to wrap up quickly.

I was mistaken.

About this time, I start to hear this little *blip, blip, blip* in my right ear. It sounded very familiar. I suppose he could see the puzzled look on my face.

He said, "Don't worry, that's just the sonar. I'm using a sonar system to help me locate the other two canals in your tooth."

Well, you could have brought out the Long Island Medium to assist me and still I would have never guessed this. Sonar? I thought that's what you used to locate battleships or sunken treasure.

In a space no bigger in diameter than a pencil, which contains four canals, you are telling me you need sonar? Couldn't you just maybe try a millionth of an inch to the left, or a half-a-millionth of an inch to the right? I was wondering how he could find his way home.

This *blip, blip, blip* sound immediately took me back a decade or so when Malaysian Flight 370 went down somewhere and was never seen or heard from again. I watched with tremendous interest for days as they tracked the various *blip, blip, blip* sounds that they hoped were originating from the black box of that aircraft. It seemed there were hours of newscasts with the *blip, blip, blip* going on continuously in the background. I became pretty obsessed with the news coverage.

While searching for Malaysian Flight 370, sonar would pick up some faint blips and the team would think it might be the downed jet. They would send search crews, just to discover it was a submarine or some other erroneous source, but never the aircraft in question.

Experts reconstructed flight patterns, tracked signals, and analyzed data for months with no luck. The plane simply disappeared. Vanished. Two-hundred and twenty-seven people just gone from the face of the earth without a trace.

Years-long searches of the Indian Ocean have never located the wreckage. Now, it is believed the pilot intentionally downed the flight—which seems to be the only logical explanation. But there are still so many other theories. It is still, in my opinion, one of the great mysteries of my lifetime.

Funny the things that go through your mind when someone is using a sonar device inside your tooth.

As for the root canal, it was inconvenient, but not painful. I did look like a stroke victim for the rest of the day after he loaded me up with novocaine. Other than that, I had no side effects.

The torn retina was a bit more stressful.

This doctor was in a very modern, newly renovated office. He was one of a large group of retina specialists, and they operated in a maze of sleek, minimalistic exam and testing rooms. My doctor was young, and he moved very quickly with his diagnosis and treatment. I was hardly there any time before I was moved into a room for laser surgery.

He had downplayed the surgery so much that I wasn't really worried. I had many friends who had cataracts removed and others that had LASIK surgery, and none acted as if it was a big deal. So this comforted me.

Being wide awake as he was sticking needles in my eye wasn't so bad. It didn't even bother me when he started welding-down this tear in my eye, with a machine-gun sounding laser. I got used to it quickly. Although it was uncomfortable, I could tolerate it. Going blind in that eye when the laser started was more disconcerting than anything, closely followed by the burning smell and the extremely bright flashes of light in my other eye.

It was all quite intense and it went on longer than I expected. It was, however, over soon enough. I was so thankful to have caught it before the retina detached, which he said would have been a much more complicated surgery and recovery.

High Maintenance

The worst part of the whole procedure happened on the follow-up visit.

They took all these pictures of the inside of my eye where the repair had been done. Then they put them all up on a screen in the exam room for me to review. One quick glance was plenty for me, but the doctor wanted to dwell on them, and point out all the work he had done. He wanted me to study the photos along with him. This was literally making me gag. If you think I am joking, take a look at some photos of the inside of your eye. It's pretty gross.

I thought about how ironic it would be to make it through the eye surgery with ease and then literally throw-up looking at the photos.

But that's kind of the way I am.

Things that scare some people—like needles and tests and such—don't usually bother me. It's the visual things that get to me, like looking at the photos of the inside of my eye.

Or like the unsettled feeling I get from sitting in poorly decorated waiting rooms, or laying in a dental chair and having stuffed animals watch me from a thirty-year-old fake ficus tree, as a sonar *blips* in my ear, looking for a root canal.

Truth in Advertising

Oprah. Remember her? Yes, that Oprah. The one with the hugely successful talk show back in the '90s and early 2000s. Over her many years on the air she asked lots of thought-provoking questions of her guests, but my favorite question she asked was this: "What do you know for sure?"

Every once in a while I ask that question of myself and, I hate to say it, but if I am really honest—not much.

The older I get, the less sure I am about anything. And as I sit here racking my brain, I can barely come up with anything that I know—absolutely—for sure.

Except for one thing. There is one thing I am sure about. And that is this: the Magic Eraser is indeed magical.

No doubt about it.

That little mystical, magical, weightless, piece of white foam can take a stain off of anything. And I do mean anything.

It can remove stains of all kinds from painted walls without removing the paint underneath. The Magic Eraser has saved me from having to repaint entire rooms. It can also take the gunk off my glass stovetop and the soap scum off of my glass shower doors. It will even restore the dirty discolored soles on my tennis shoes to a shade of white. Not perfectly white like brand new, but at least a nice shade of off-white. Nothing else I've tried on them before has come close.

Honestly, I haven't found anything that it can't do. If not perfectly well, at least pretty well.

I remember back in the '90s, there was a big to-do about microfiber cloths. They were touted as the magical cleaning products of their day. But as far as I am concerned, microfiber was the big lie. I found them to be a huge disappointment. All they did was spread the dirt all around and never collect it.

They weren't nearly as effective as the magical dust cloths my mom used to buy at the hardware store. These were mustard yellow felt-like cloths with a kind of oily finish. They were also magical. I think they were actually called magic dust cloths at one time. But they only had one use, and that was for dusting, so they never really got the recognition they deserved. They did however magically—or maybe magnetically—almost suck the dust off of whatever needed dusting. I loved them. You can still find them online. They are made by Guardsman and called dusting cloths, I believe. And they are still the only dust cloths I use.

These yellow cloths would eventually have to be washed because they would collect so much dust that the dust magnet would be neutralized. Every time you washed them, the magical qualities would return, but become less and less effective over time. Kind of like how Aunt Clara's magical powers faded on *Bewitched*. Magic Erasers literally disintegrate during use, and won't last for more than a few cleaning sessions. So they aren't absolutely perfect either. But they sure are close.

After the let-down of microfiber, I was truly skeptical when I first began hearing ads for the Magic Eraser. In protest of what I felt sure was false advertising, I didn't buy one for years. I just could not believe that a little foam pad could be any better than all the other various sponges and wool pads I had used over the years. Since I had little success with those, I was convinced this was just another slick advertising campaign with little substance to back it up.

But finally, after hearing about them from my painter of all people, I decided to give one a try. I cannot tell you how stunned I was. It really, really worked. I could easily wipe black marks off of walls that had been there for years. It truly was magic, and I fell deeply in love. I've bought extra boxes and keep them handy at all times.

A few years ago, I installed new white quartz countertops in my condo, and it seemed every time I put something down on them, a black streak appeared. I couldn't figure out what was causing the marks. They just seemed to come from nowhere, no matter how gentle I was with them—and lord knows they weren't occurring due to pot and pan usage.

I tried everything. Stone cleaners and other types of cleaning solutions wouldn't do a thing. No matter how hard I scrubbed they would not go away. So, when I discovered the Magic Eraser, I gave that a try.

Truth in Advertising

I just dampened the sponge with water and scrubbed some, and *poof*, no more black streaks. Amazing. I couldn't stop the streaks from appearing, but I could sure get rid of them easily.

Every time I think I have exhausted all the possible uses for them, I find a new one. Sometimes for cleaning, and sometimes for something totally unexpected.

A few years ago, one of my worst nightmares came true. I was invited to a sixtieth-birthday party—a pool party. If you know me, you know that I don't do pools, or shorts, or any combination of the two. I am super pale and super tall and therefore look like a huge neon-white ghost in the water. I have horrible flashbacks of childhood ridicule and torment at the pool.

I decided that I would use some self-tanner to at least reduce the glow of my white skin. I had used some in the past when I went on cruises and it worked fairly well—if you didn't look too close. Instead of the lotion I had previously used, this time, I bought a spray-on tanner. It was highly rated and seemed easier to apply. So I sprayed on a light coat the day before the party. I'd been burned before—no pun intended— and knew to start out light with these products.

Yes, I know I was cutting it close.

But after the required three hours, I looked, and couldn't tell it had done one thing. My white skin was still glowing. I figured I must not have sprayed on a heavy enough coating. I waited a few more hours and still nothing. So, I decided to spray on another light coating that evening before bed.

Imagine my surprise when I woke up the next morning and looked at my legs.

They were streaked and striped. I looked like a zebra.

A light-tan and brown zebra.

Apparently, the first layer of color didn't appear on me until much later than the predicted three hours. So, the first coating was the lighter tan and then the areas that got the second coating were the stripes. My legs were a thing of beauty—in *no* way, from any angle. I'm not sure you could have replicated this pattern if you tried.

But now it was just hours before the party and I really needed to show up. Then I remembered the scene in the movie *The Wedding Planner* when a bride overdoes the self-tanner and comes to Jennifer Lopez in hysterics. Jennifer, the wedding planner, replies, "Lemon juice and a loofa, and scrub, scrub, scrub."

Well, I didn't have a loofa or lemon juice. But then it hit me: I had a magic eraser.

So I took one out, and scrubbed, scrubbed, scrubbed. And you know what. It worked. It sort of evened out the color and removed the dark streaks. It probably removed a top layer of skin too, but that was ok. I hear exfoliation is good. And who knows, I might have erased a few early skin cancers in the process.

Trust me when I say this, it was not perfect, not by a long shot. I still was not even-toned, but at least I could show up to the party, no longer white as a ghost, and no longer striped. The Magic Eraser had, once again, saved the day.

I'm sure there are some of you reading this that will disagree with me. Obviously, some of you must like those irritating microfiber cleaning products because they sell a ton of them. And some of you — misguided as you could possibly be — might go as far as to say you don't like the Magic Eraser. But I need to be honest, and I'm not going to sugar-coat it.

You are wrong.

Seriously wrong.

Some things are worth taking a stand for, and this is one of them.

The Magic Eraser is truly magical, and I have no doubt about that.

I'M NOT SO EXCITED

I hope, before I die, something excites me enough to want to paint a big, blue, capital letter on my chest, and stand at an outdoor sporting event, arms locked with my friends, to form a phrase like "GO BIG DAWGS."

I would so love to feel the sheer joy these guys seem to get from standing there in the bleachers — shirtless on national television at some college playoff game — screaming obscenities at the other team. If the temperatures are below freezing, even better.

I can only imagine the rush they feel as part of a brotherhood of letter-clad shirtless men. They look as if they are having the time of their lives.

I can imagine them talking about it for years to come. Getting together at class reunions and standing in the same line-up once again, maybe raising their shirts to expose their now-inflated bellies for a revelatory Facebook photo, marking the twentieth anniversary of that fun-filled cold day. I imagine them still talking about it in their seventies, and even in the nursing home.

But it doesn't end there.

These sports enthusiasts have a lifetime of sports-related memories like that. Their sporting journey begins in their grade-school years, playing first on Little League teams and travel ball teams, then middle school football, then high school football and basketball. They live for it and they love it.

Through the years, some of the athletes fall away, and lose interest in sports. They might begin to pursue other interests, like travel or do-it-yourself projects. The hard-core sports lovers might enjoy those too, but for them sports always take priority, whether it is professional sports, college sports, or their children's sporting activities.

I can't say this with any level of certainty, but I'd just bet that many of the Little League coaches that become irate, and get thrown out of their children's games, once sported a big blue capital letter on their chest.

It always fascinates me, this dedication and exhilaration that sports bring about. I sit in awe when I catch a glimpse of these college football games, with a stadium packed-full of over a hundred-thousand rabid fans. They are sitting on miserably tiny, cramped, hard, metal seats, freezing in foul winter weather, and having the time of their lives.

They are all dressed in the team colors too. They don't just have one jersey to wear to the game either. They have an entire wardrobe of clothes, emblazoned with team logos, in bright polyester school colors, for all seasons, all sports, and all events.

They want everyone to know who they are rooting for: their team.

I say *their* team, because that's what the fans say.

They are possessive. If the Tennessee Vols beat Bama, they never say, "The Vols won last weekend."

They say, "We won last weekend." Or "We scored a touchdown with six seconds to go," or "We barely eked out a win in overtime."

They are not only dedicated supporters, they claim complete ownership of the team.

It doesn't matter if they attended the university or not—most of them didn't. These followers lay claim to it, and hang on until the bitter end of every game. Their loyalty outlives high school sweethearts, college flings, and even marriages. It is true devotion, and lasting.

Unfortunately, I can never in my lifetime remember feeling anything as euphoric as how these enthusiasts must feel when their team wins a playoff game—not to mention a national title. They are on cloud nine, and relive the game moment-by-moment for years to come. They talk about the national title *we* won, and what the chances are that *we* will win another.

But who is this *we*? As far as I could see, your team had only eleven players on the field when the winning touchdown was scored. Hearing the fans tell it, you'd think they were on the field too, running the ball into the end zone.

See, I don't really play sports or watch them. I'm pretty good at Ping-Pong, and I did play tennis years ago, but I sort of let that slip away. So does that even count? I think not. I still enjoy watching a tennis match now and then, but honestly if that were all gone tomorrow, and professional tennis no longer existed, I wouldn't really miss it.

That kind of makes me sad too, because I do remember feeling some excitement for tennis. On my first trip to London I even made the trek all the way out to Wimbledon to see the famous center court. So I must have been pretty emotionally involved with the sport at that time, but the real excitement I used to feel for tennis is gone.

Maybe it's genetic. Both my parents are of German ancestry. And if you look up common traits of German people—like I just did—you see descriptive words like creative, focused, disciplined, hardworking, efficient and reserved. Nothing like excitable, free-spirited or fun-loving is mentioned.

Or maybe it's in the stars. Maybe I wasn't born under the right sign. I'm a Cancer. Yes, I know, sounds depressing, doesn't it? Cancers are thought to be compassionate, loyal, loving and sensitive. Again, it doesn't say a thing about being free-spirited or filled with enthusiasm.

I think I have the wrong genetics and the wrong sign. This is looking worse by the moment.

How do you get those highs? I don't do drugs or drink, but surely those aren't necessary to feel the passion for sports that some people feel. I wonder if they are that passionate about everything, or just sports. Do they focus on their job with the same intense interest they devote to a game? Do they parent that way? Sure, I know the majority of those attending the games are probably drinking some, or maybe a lot. But they are sober at work on Monday morning when they are recounting every moment of the game with their friends. Their excitement level is no less on Monday morning than it was on game day.

So my *not* drinking doesn't seem to be the issue.

Their emotions are just as extreme if the game is lost: the devotees are lower than low. Some can hardly function they are so depressed. They experience the deepest lows of the team as well. The mood of these zealots, throughout football season, is tied directly to the win-loss record of their chosen team.

You know what it sounds like—the elevated moods, the high-highs, and the low-lows. It sounds like some of the main symptoms of bipolar disorder. But that doesn't make sense. Being bipolar is a serious, life-altering disorder with no choice. Sports fans *want* to experience these highs and lows. They sign up for it, and return to it again and again, even when they swear-off after their team continues to have losing seasons.

I've spent my life around people of all ages, walks-of-life, income, and education levels, and I still don't see any rhyme or reason for who gets into this sports zone—this passion-filled co-existence with a team. But I never thought to check their sign, or their ancestry. Maybe I've stumbled upon something.

Some of this team-loyalty is handed-down through generations. Or some people adopt a team because they find a particular player charismatic. Or they live in the home city of the team, and then count themselves a member of that team for the rest of their lives. They become immersed in it and become die-hard supporters.

But how do you get to that ultimate level, where you make sacrifices for your team? I not talking about the supportive fans that attend games when they can but don't think it earth-shaking if they can't.

The fans I am talking about are the ones that plan their vacations around the away games, and they either attend or have parties to watch all the home games. They have rooms in their homes decorated with their team's memorabilia, and movie-theater-size screens to watch every punt and every pass. They will get mad if you try to talk to them during the action. They will offend friends and ask them to leave if the friend stands in front of the screen.

These are the ones that make me a bit jealous. Because I can think of nothing that excites me that much. Not ever.

The closest thing I can equate it to is my going to a play or a concert. I do get excited if I am going to see a great artist perform or a show I really enjoy. I love the theater and I relish a great performance. I think about it for weeks, or sometimes even years after. I think about the music, the writing, the staging and the sets. But I know I am just observing. I never take ownership of it. I never see myself as part of the team like football fans do.

You would never hear me say, "I saw this great new show called *Dear Evan Hansen* last night, and we gave the best performance. We literally killed, and we got three standing ovations."

No matter how much I love a show, I can't claim the performance like a you can a sports event. Maybe that's why there is such pleasure in sports. Because in your mind, you did something, you won. You cheered your team on, and *we* won. You played a part.

It's not just sports, either. Taylor Swift and Beyoncé literally boosted the entire economy with their massively popular tours. People are traveling around the globe to see one of their shows. Their fans are as rabid as the sports followers. These music zealots buy special outfits and plan vacations around attending one of these concerts. Swifties will fly to Tokyo or Australia to see the concert if they can't get tickets in the USA, or they might fly there to see the concert a second or a third time.

I can understand this to a degree. I love concerts. But once again, these folks are operating on another level. Many of them seem all-consumed by their love for their artist. It amazes me.

I've certainly felt passion for many of my favorite artists. No doubt. I've flown to New York to see a particular show or a concert that I really wanted to see. I've driven to other cities—within a reasonable radius of my home—to see concerts, too. But I have never, ever considered clipping those little flags on my car windows to display my team's logo, or painted "Barry Manilow Bound" on my car window with shoe polish to announce where I was going.

The thought of flying twenty-four hours, around the world, just to see a concert, is something I cannot fathom. I just don't have it in me. I don't think I ever did.

So I accept it. I don't jump up and down. I don't yell for teams. I don't wear their jerseys.

And I have also come to accept that I'll never have those memories, and I'll probably never have that level of enthusiasm for anything.

Well, ok, maybe if I wrote a play and it made it to a Broadway stage. Check back with me then. I might be jumping up and down. I might be screaming.

I'm Not So Excited

This, however, is highly unlikely to happen—the play and the screaming.

I like to think that some things do really impact me, and they find a deep place in my soul and stay with me for a lifetime. Actually, I know they do. I just register them differently. Somewhere inside they resonate, and they give me joy. Some of them might be talked about at a reunion or at a dinner with friends, and some of them might even make it into a story.

The best memories though, I usually just keep to myself. Maybe it's the German in me. I'm fairly even keeled, and maybe a bit stoic on the outside, and I guess that will have to be ok. I know it isn't going to change now. I'll just register my big wins—and my big losses—inside. Out of public scrutiny. No big capital blue letter on my chest needed.

But just in case:

GO BIG DAWGS.

GOOD MORNING, DOLLY

Every once in a while I wake up at some crazy-early hour like 4 a.m., and I can't go back to sleep. I toss and turn for a while, and then I think about how my day will be ruined, and how I'll be yawning all afternoon if I can't get a couple more hours of sleep.

Luckily, I usually can drift back to sleep. But before I do I usually have a harrowing thought: some people intentionally get up at this time. Not to watch the sunrise, or because they have to get to the airport for an early flight to somewhere amazing. No. They wake up at this ungodly hour to go to the gym and work out. They are literally at the gym and ready to exercise by 4:30 a.m. and complaining that the YMCA doesn't open earlier.

People tell me about these gym habits a lot. "Oh, I am up and at the gym every morning by 5 a.m." Like it's something to be proud of. I want to ask why in the world they would do that.

You can tell they feel superior because of their early-morning rising and working-out before I ever get out of bed. I hear the gym is full at 5 a.m. and that's just fine with me. Let them all get done and out of my way. They are probably also running 10Ks on the weekend and doing a lot of skiing and water sports. My body just isn't up for that. It never has been—even as a child.

I told my trainer that I have been preserving my body—my entire life—for old age. I simply did not want to take a chance of wearing out my knees and hips and other joints doing crazy stuff like running twenty-six miles in one morning. So far it has paid off. As of today, I still have all my original parts. But the day is young. I could always break a hip on the way to the car.

I do exercise, and I walk a lot, so it's not like I am a total slug. But talking to these people, you would surely think that I am.

I do feel quite accomplished, though, in one thing: sleeping.

Sleeping is something that I am really good at. I would go so far as to say I excel at it. Especially when I was younger. My mother had a terrible time waking me up for school. She would yell and yell at me to get up and I would put it off until the very last minute.

I love sleeping. It's the best. I like to get at least eight hours of sleep every night, and nine is even better.

These days I do wake up more often during the night, but even though sometimes it takes some time I usually can get back to sleep. At least I always try. This is another area where I feel people are very confused or just plain nuts. People will tell me, "Oh, I woke up at 4 a.m. and couldn't go back to sleep, so I just got up and headed into the office."

Trust me on this: I have never, ever done that.

I think they are just not trying hard enough to go

Good Morning, Dolly

back to sleep. They should put more effort into it. I know they'd be glad they did. Anyway I have no idea what I would do if I got up at 4 a.m. but I sure wouldn't go to the office. And I know I would not go to the gym either.

I read an article the other day that made me smile. It also made me really want to share it with all the overbearing 4 a.m. gym bunnies. It was about Dolly Parton.

I always thought she must be superhuman to get all the things accomplished that she does. And I was right. She said she never sleeps later than 3 a.m. She said she loves to get up early just like her Daddy did and get some work done, maybe meditate, write a song or two, and then cook breakfast for her husband all before 5 a.m.

I've never been a country music fan at all, but I do like Dolly Parton. I've always liked her. I think it's the fact that she's unapologetically herself and completely authentic. It amazes me that she always seems to be in a good mood. To me it appears her clothes are very tight, and you'd think they must be binding and uncomfortable. I get cranky when my waistband is even a little bit snug.

You'd think she would be miserable, sitting for hours doing interviews and promoting her latest projects. I think doing interviews and promos all day would be miserable even in pajamas, but you'd never know if she is. She never complains and always has a great attitude. She just puts on her next tight, corseted outfit, changes her wig, and goes to the next talk show.

I find it funny to look back at some of the old clips

of Barbara Walters interviewing Dolly. It's obvious that Barbara Walters feels a bit superior and is trying to make Dolly feel foolish for wearing her wigs and makeup and gaudy outfits, but Dolly remains calm and cool. Dolly bluntly dresses Barbara down, explaining that she is in control of her image, and knows exactly what she is doing, and is no dumb blonde. Barbara Walters quickly realizes she has met her equal.

It seems to me that since the death of Betty White, Dolly has now become America's most-loved senior citizen. She's an unlikely choice, since these days she's showing more cleavage than a nineteen-year-old on spring break, but she's a good choice I think, and the kind of role model I can get behind.

It's amazing to me that, in her sixty-plus-year career, Dolly has never really made a misstep. She's always made the right choices for herself, and has been overwhelmingly successful in her music and philanthropic endeavors. Authenticity is her key to success I believe. She is the perfect antidote for a world in which people do anything and everything to gain social media followers. She's living proof that if you remain true to yourself, do your own thing, and do it well, the followers will come to you. And they have.

It's hard to believe that it's real, that one person can be all these things to all these people, but she really is. Recently, my friend Renee was staying in one of Dolly's hotels in Dollywood with her husband and daughter. They ran into Dolly in the hall of the hotel. Just as you would hope, Dolly came up to them, asked if they wanted photos, posed with them, and then spent some time talking as if she had nothing else to do—when you know she probably had fifty things on her schedule.

My favorite Dolly story is one that Julia Roberts told in an interview after the making of the movie *Steel Magnolias*. Roberts said that one day, during filming in New Orleans, she and the other leading ladies were all sitting around on the set. It was hot, and everyone was complaining about how miserable they were—everyone except Dolly.

Julia said Dolly was sitting there in her wig, and makeup, and costume, and never complained once. When Julia asked her why she wasn't complaining about the heat like everyone else, Dolly responded with a classic Dolly line. She said, "When I was a little girl all I ever wanted was to be rich and famous, and now I am both of those, and I'm certainly not going to complain about it."

I think that just says so much about her work ethic, her gratitude, and life in general.

So, for all of you that think making it to the gym by 5 a.m. is a big deal, I'm really not that impressed. Just remember that Dolly has already been up, put on her makeup and a wig, written a hit song or two, planned a new attraction for her theme park, and scrambled eggs for Carl Dean—all long before you've lifted your first dumbbell.

Airmail and Chocolate Pie

I talk about it a lot—it's hard not to. The swift passage of time, and the current that seems to propel it, is constant.

I get to the office on Monday thinking about all the things I want to accomplish that week. Within an eye-blink, it seems I am walking out of the office on Friday wondering why I got so little done.

In 2023, I watched the days of June flit by, swiftly passing the twentieth anniversary of my mother's death.

Thoughts of my mother had been with me more and more, and the anniversary marking two decades since her death was a bit hard to take. Twenty years since I spoke to her, or heard her voice, or laughed at any of her sharp remarks.

I've written about her. Actually, quite a lot. I've published some of those stories. Some I have not. Too personal to let go of just yet.

She always fascinated me. She did not have an easy life. Not at all. She grew up poor, on a typical country farm, in rural Middle Tennessee, with little other than the bare necessities.

I could always tell there were many dark clouds in the memories of her youth. She had seen true hardship. Like most of that greatest generation, she had to be tough. She had been born during the early days of the Great Depression, lost a sibling to diphtheria in infancy, survived an almost-lethal snake bite, and lived her teenage years under the threat of World War II. She watched as friends and cousins and school mates went to war—many to never return. No wonder she never talked about her childhood. It was during a time of great sacrifice and very simple pleasures—if pleasures were to be found at all. It was filled with adult experiences whether she was ready for them or not.

I can remember feeling the threat of the Vietnam War during my grade school years, and the fear of being drafted. Fortunately for me, the draft, and the war, ended before I became the eligible age. That was the only experience I could, in some way, relate to hers—and it paled by comparison.

Beyond all of that though, there was always a sense that I just didn't know her in the way I really wanted to. When my mother was diagnosed with cancer, I didn't want to think of her dying as a reality. I tried to convince myself she would survive. She was too young to die. Too tough to die. But as the cancer ate away at her, little by little, the realization that she actually would die sank in.

Questions did come to me, things I wanted to ask her. But every time I was with her alone, I knew that asking them would be an unwanted clue—a clue that I was preparing for her death.

This was something I could not do.

I didn't want—in any way—to make her feel I was preparing for life without her. First of all, because I wanted to do everything possible to build up her resolve and strength. I wanted her to keep fighting. Secondly, I really didn't want to acknowledge it myself. I couldn't let myself prepare for the end.

I think we all felt that way. No one wanted to talk about it. But as time passed and treatments failed to work, the reality began to sink in. I could sense that she was ready to go. She even told me so one day. After a last round of chemo failed to produce any results, the doctors said they had nothing else to try. Mom was stoic and, I think, already resolved to stop the treatments even if they had more to offer. She was exhausted.

So somewhere between that doctor's visit and our arrival back home, she told me that she was ready to go. She was tired of it all. The treatments, the doctors, the battle. Looking back, I think that would have been the time to ask a lot of those questions. But I was trying to hold it together. You see, I am not as tough as she.

My questions weren't invasive or emotionally charged. Just simple things, like how long she and Dad dated before they got married. And how did they first meet? Or what was her favorite subject in high school, and her favorite teacher? Who did she hang out with? When did she move to town? Did they ever go to a concert or see many movies? Just simple things. Simple things that all happened before I knew her.

My earliest memories of any conversations with her were probably when I was eight or so, and I remember very little about those. Mom was thirty-four when she had me, so she would have been in her early forties when I was in the third grade. But I was surprised how little I really knew about her day-to-day life, her life as a young woman.

So many of these thoughts were with me—popping into my mind now and then—during that twentieth year after her death. I wanted to investigate some. But there was no one to ask. All of her friends had passed, and my aunt, her younger sister, was suffering with dementia. I felt that I would just have to live with the information I had. Be content with it.

Then this thing called fate steps in.

I've always heard that fate steps in at key moments, and in this case I would have to agree.

Fate sort of did step in with my design career and propelled me into a lifetime of creative work.

And fate definitely lent a hand with my writing. It was as simple as an email. An email, out of the blue during COVID, from an old friend. She asked me if she could read some of my old stories. The email did its job and prompted me to dig out those old stories and share them once more. And that prompted me to start writing again.

So, as I was remembering all those unanswered questions about my mom, there was yet another stroke of fate. And this time, it was much more direct.

I have never experienced such an on-target—and needed—delivery of fate. I got something I didn't even know to wish for. Something I didn't even know existed. Something so simple, yet mind-boggling.

I got my mother's words. Thousands of them.

Someone had found an old duffle bag of my dad's. It was in a shed on what was once the old Evers' family farm. My dad's brother had continued to farm there and lived on the property until he died. After my uncle died—I'm not sure what year exactly—they sold the old Evers' family farm. The new owners found my dad's old duffle bag in a shed. They called my nephew, and my nephew called me.

Apparently, when my dad got out of the Air Force, he stored this duffle bag in that shed. And it had been there ever since. Amazingly, in that old duffle bag was every letter that my father received during his time in the military.

There were hundreds of letters. Letters from his friends and his family, but mostly, from my mom. Hundreds of handwritten letters. They weren't married at the time, only dating. I'm not sure how long they had dated before he went into the Air Force —not for very long I think—but they kept in close touch all during his deployment. Thankfully, they both wrote to each other a lot.

My nephews were excited too. They had been especially close to my mother, and they only knew her as a sixty-something-year-old woman. They had heard a few stories of her youth, but not that many. They, too, had lots of questions they wished they had asked her.

Mom just never talked about herself. She didn't think her life was interesting enough to talk about. So finding these letters from 1951, '52, '53, and '54— letters containing thousands and thousands of her words telling the stories of those days—was epic. I was gobsmacked, to say the least.

She would have been in her early to mid twenties at the time they were written. I knew she was working at the First National Bank then, and living in town with her aunts, but I didn't know much more about that time in her life.

So here I am in 2024, reading these letters one by one—these little gems—filled with the details about her days.

Chills.

Now reading these letters feels as if, in a way, I'm meeting my mom again, as a young woman. I'm meeting her before she became a mother and a caregiver and all those things that bring on maturity and seriousness.

When I was a child, and first knew my mom, she had so many family responsibilities, she hardly had time for fun. She was always so busy. In a hurry. Going to the grocery, or taking someone to the doctor, or checking on a sick neighbor. Then, of course, there were three meals a day to be prepared, and lots and lots of family laundry to do. No Pampers back then either, even the diapers had to be laundered. Her parents were also having health issues at this time, and she was doing a lot to help them.

I remember her working hard most all the time, and always taking care of all of us. It was a big job: a husband, three children, and not much help. She never had girls' nights, or dinners out, or movie nights. Maybe a home-demonstration club meeting once a month, but that was about it. So it's no surprise she never talked about favorite songs, or movies, or going to a dance. Those things were low on her list of priorities, and seldom done.

This was the life all of her friends had back then, too.

All these southern, Catholic mothers with children, who had husbands who brought in the family paycheck but didn't help with any chores at home. This was a different time. The men were the head of the house, and their word usually went. Mom never complained and seemed to be content in her role as a wife and mother.

But here, in these letters, she talks about her life as a single and self-sufficient woman. The only period in her life when she got to do exactly what she wanted and had few responsibilities. She speaks of her life and her siblings, and doing things with her aunt and with friends. She talks about seeing movies, listening to music, attending the high school basketball games, going on a few trips, and all those fun things I wasn't sure she ever got to do as a young person. She even mentions going to square dances at the K.C. Club. I never knew.

And best of all—the very best of all—she speaks of spending a lot of time with Lorena. Lorena and her brother Joe were my two favorite people, other than my parents, from my childhood. I've written about them in my first book. I adored them. They were fun and joyful and kind, and I miss them both to this day. They were my parents' best friends throughout my childhood.

I never knew for sure when Lorena and Joe came into her life, but now I am finding out that Mom met Lorena long before she was married to Dad. In one letter, Mom mentions going by to give Lorena a home perm after work. In another letter, going to a chocolate-pie party at Lorena's house. I haven't seen anything in the letters yet about Joe. I'm hoping for an update on him. I know he served in the military and that's probably why he isn't mentioned at any of these gatherings, but I'd like to know for sure.

Reading about these things makes me so happy — these simple things like a pie party. I can't think of anything in this world I'd rather do right now than go to a chocolate-pie party with my mom and Lorena. I dearly love chocolate pie, and I can't think of any better company than would have been found at that party. Mom's Aunt Louise was probably there too — she and Lorena were close — and maybe some others. I can just see them now, laughing and joking and talking about their day. In that letter Mom said, "That Lorena sure is a swell cook," and I remember that very well myself. Oh, to taste that pie. To be in that conversation. Even though I wasn't there, it makes me so happy that my mother was able to have those experiences.

Sadly, I am finding out in Mom's updates that Lorena was already having vision problems at this time. She had vision problems all during the years I knew her, but I had no idea when they had begun. In the letters, Mom told Dad about Lorena's many trips to Nashville for various eye surgeries. There were multiple surgeries and a bad eye infection. In one of the later letters, Mom explains to Dad that Lorena had completely lost vision in her right eye for good. She probably was around forty years old. Lorena never complained though. Even years later when she was my babysitter and was having vision problems in her other eye, she still didn't complain.

Lorena never married. Her time was spent taking

care of her mother who was bed-ridden, and babysitting for kids in the neighborhood. Her life was not easy, but you would have never known it. She was pure joy. Her brother Joe never married either and they shared the family home. Later when Mom and Dad married, Joe and Lorena came to our house every Saturday night. My brother and sister and I loved those nights.

There were also letters to my dad from his buddies, who were also serving overseas. A couple of my dad's friends, from Boonetown, had enlisted at the same time, and they kept in contact while serving.

When I was young, Dad often talked about how he and his buddies would try to get together for some trips when they were all able to meet. The trip Dad talked about most was their trip to Paris. The three of them met there, in Paris, for a little getaway, and Dad had lots of photos and fond memories from that trip. Throughout his life, Dad kept in touch with one of his friends, Mike, from that trip. They continued to travel together with their wives in their later years. And in those later years, Mike created a video of that trip to Paris, using all of their photos and with background music from the movie An American in Paris—coincidentally about an American soldier in Paris.

It just occurred to me that my oldest brother was named Mike as well. I wonder if that was a hat-tip to Dad's old buddy?

Several times in her letters, Mom mentions the stories Dad had told her about some of these trips and how she wants to hear more of the details when they see each other in person. I am sure that the Paris trip was one of those. Considering that my mother had never traveled anywhere much, these trips in Europe must have sounded quite spectacular to her.

Dad must have asked Mom to write to him more often in one of his letters because Mom writes back apologizing, explaining how she feels that she has nothing much of interest to talk about. At least when compared to his trips and military assignments. But she assures him that he is always on her mind. She promises to write more often.

Sadly, I don't think Mom realized how comforting those little ordinary stories about her day, her friends, and her family would be to him when he was so far away from home and wishing desperately to be back there. It's always the simple things, I think, that you miss the most, and I feel sure that was true for my dad.

I am sure he found enjoyment in some of the places he was seeing and the new friends he made, but when you are far from home there is always the yearning for words from the people who have known you the longest and that love you the most. Mom, being Mom, never gave herself enough credit.

But she deserved credit for being mature and smart. She was a twenty-five-ish single woman, living in a town where most of her friends were already married with two or three children. I am sure she was being asked all the time when she would be next. She must have felt a lot pressure to do the same.

In the letters, it is obvious they are in love, and they tell each other so, and sometimes they are a bit flirtatious. But this was a proper romance. In one of the early letters, Mom responds to Dad's proposal that they marry in 1955. This was four years in the future and a long time to wait. Mom replies that she would love to marry him if they still feel the same way then.

It's obvious from that letter that my mother never pressured my dad to get married. She tells him that whatever is meant to be, will be. She doesn't hint about getting married sooner—on one of his leaves— or try to rush things. They even agree to see other people if they feel they need to, and they agree to move forward cautiously. I could imagine a lot of women at that age pushing hard for a wedding ring once a proposal had been offered. Not her.

In that fate-filled duffle bag, there were letters about the weather, and church, and nothing much at all, as well as letters with family updates and news of friends getting married and having children. There were also Christmas cards and birthday cards and notes from his brothers, sisters and friends. But mainly the letters from my mom. So many letters from her.

As of this writing, I haven't read all of the letters. I'm savoring them. I also wanted to write this story as it is unfolding. I want to always remember this feeling of excitement and unexpected bliss as I immerse myself in my parents' early life.

Now, I read a few pages and then try to let those images gel in my brain. I try to imagine myself at those gatherings with some of the best people I ever knew. I imagine my mother being so surprised and happy to see her brother walk into the bank, unannounced, after being away in the military for so long. I visualize the story just as she told it in one letter. Then, in the next lines, I hear her assuring my dad that she would be even happier to see him walk in and surprise her.

Or I imagine her with Lorena, Aunt Louise, and her other buddies, having dinner and eating chocolate pie. Sitting around that kitchen table, laughing and talking, maybe about my dad and what the future might hold for the two of them.

While she was writing those letters, her future was wide open—unwritten. My mom was, for the only time in her life, an independent woman. She seemed to be happy, living in town in her little rented room, enjoying life. She was making friends, working, and writing letters. Writing lots and lots of letters to her sweetheart—her sweetheart overseas, serving his country. It was the stuff of so many movies of that time.

But this wasn't a movie. This was real life, and this was the precursor to my life. Because they did get married, in 1955, just as he had asked, after he got out of the Air Force. It did work out as it was meant to. They were married for forty-eight years.

I am cherishing these words on these brittle yellowed pages. These letters from her, sent across the sea with a six-cent purple airmail stamp. Not written to me, but, in some way, seemingly sent just to me. To answer my questions.

The joy I feel at hearing her words, her thoughts, and her humor is so satisfying.

I know—this time for sure—these are the last words of hers I will hear. This moment of serendipity, twenty years after her death, is something most people never get, so I'm ever grateful for it.

I'm very grateful, too, that these last memories of her are happy ones. They aren't filled with doctor visits and chemotherapy treatments and hair loss. They are of her in her prime, when things were possible, and the future was yet to be written.

I'm grateful that someone kept that duffle bag and returned it to our family.

I'm grateful to fill in some blanks and to think of her smiling, savoring every bite of chocolate pie.

I'm grateful to remember what a great person she was.

And I'm grateful she was my mom.

Airmail and Chocolate Pie

Dr. Karma

I'm sure this never happens to most people.

Other people can't be this crazy.

But sometimes this thing happens to me, and it makes me so mad.

It starts when I've been sick and suffering dreadfully with something, like a killer pain in my back, or a really bad case of the flu. Then I finally decide that it's not going away without medical intervention. So I make an appointment with my doctor. Of course, you can't ever get in to see a doctor the day you need them the most. There is usually a day or two—or more—of a delay.

Then, just as sure as the world, on the day of my doctor visit, my symptoms are suddenly much better. Sure, you want to feel better, but not on the day of your appointment. On that day I still want to feel sick and look terrible.

Then I'm in a quandary. What should I do?

Should I cancel the appointment, or should I go? Only a couple of days before, I felt so bad that I could hardly get out of bed. My back was in severe pain and I couldn't stand up straight. I could hardly walk.

Or my throat was really sore, I was coughing constantly, and I had body aches all over.

On the day of the appointment though, I feel better. Not great, but ok. And now I have the nagging feeling that none of my symptoms will be good enough. I feel they won't stack up to the real sick people. I feel the need to exaggerate my symptoms. I want my current symptoms to reflect the pain and suffering that I have been through over the last few days. Sure, I might look better at the moment, but this is surely just one of those moments when you rally right before you are about to die.

When I finally get to the exam room, the doctor just looks at me like I am a hypochondriac. I know he has to be thinking, "What a baby!"

And then I start wondering if he thinks I am one of those people just trying to get a prescription for pain killers. I know that happens all the time, and I know the doctors are always on the lookout for those people but, trust me, it's the last thing on my mind. I do not enjoy being sick. I hate being sick. I hate going to the doctor, in general. I certainly don't want any unnecessary prescriptions.

I'm not a faker, but I always imagine my doctor is thinking just that. Will my throat still look sore enough? Will I still have a temperature?

But it never fails. I really hate it when he looks at my throat and gives me that look. You know the look. You *know* what he is thinking. "Did you really come in for this? You realize I'm busy with patients that are really sick, right?" I hate that look.

So then I go into this long explanation about how sick I was just a day and a half ago, and that I coughed my head off and I couldn't even get out of bed. *Trust me Doc, I still have this terrible lingering cough that I can't seem to control, except for this very moment when it is nowhere to be found.* I want him to understand that I was, and still am, sick and could have a major relapse at any moment.

Maybe I'm going on a vacation in a few days, and I don't want to feel this bad on an airplane. Please just make me feel better for my vacation. Maybe I need something, a steroid pack or whatever, to kick my immune system into overdrive and make me feel wonderful for my trip.

And then, I worry about karma.

Karma is the reason I don't want to inflate my symptoms. Especially where illness is concerned.

I don't want to lie and say that my throat is still killing me because I fear a continuous case of strep throat. Ten or so years ago, I had a continuous case of strep throat for thirty-six months before I had my tonsils removed. And I sure don't want that again. I am not going to tempt karma.

Especially not like the guy in the Nissan 380z at the post office in Boonetown.

Have you seen a Nissan 380z? I always look at the interior with amazement. I wonder how anyone can get out of it without assistance or a small crane. This car sits so low, that when you are seated in it, it appears you are basically laying on the ground. I've occasionally had to ride in one of those cars, and I have a tough time getting out of it. Those low-slung sports cars are difficult for me to exit, and I'm in pretty good shape.

This car had a handicap placard. A Nissan 380z.

Every morning when I went to get the mail, it was always parked in the only handicap spot.

There are many handicapped people who need that spot, going in and out of the post office. But he was there in the spot, every morning.

I began to watch, and I was amazed to see that the man that drove the car appeared to be in great shape, too. Every morning, he would hop out of the 380z like it was nothing, and then almost jog into the Post Office. I suppose he might have many hidden health issues, but he appeared to move about with great ease.

Of course, I had to wonder: why did he need the handicap space if he could get around so breezily? Maybe he just thought it was cool to park right at the door. But that is not the point of the handicap tag.

Personally, I just wouldn't have the stomach for it, parking in a handicap spot, I mean. Because of that pesky little thing: karma.

I fear karma and its revenge. I fear I would be permanently disabled by the end of the day. I certainly hope I never need a handicap tag on my car, so I sure don't want to tempt fate.

This guy obviously didn't fear karma like me. He didn't seem to worry that he might be tempting fate by parking in the handicap spot when he could walk very well.

He's dead now, so it's a moot point. He died young, too. But as I said, he didn't seem to let karma be an issue while he was alive.

Maybe he should have.

Anyway, the point is I won't park in a handicap spot.

Never.

That's not to say that I don't have an opinion about them. Because I think the whole reserved parking thing has gotten a little out of control. In this one parking lot, at one of the major lumber suppliers over in Monterey, they have so many spots reserved that an average healthy customer has to park over near the highway, and take a nice walk.

Of course, they have six or eight handicap-designated spots. But they also have spots reserved for veterans, and then some spots for expectant mothers, and mothers with small children, and several spots for contractors. Then, of course they have the spots blocked off for buggy returns, and so on.

I don't mean to sound mean-spirited because all these folks are well-deserving of dedicated spots. And I'm not jealous, really, I'm not. I am happy to walk because I can.

But this is a place that sells a lot of very heavy stuff. And you have to get it to your car somehow. Sometimes I get in a hurry and don't want to go get my car and bring it to the front door to pick up my stuff. So I do something stupid, like try to carry it all the way to my car.

By the time I've walked the distance of a football field carrying three fifty-pound boxes of ceramic tile to get to the only undesignated parking spot in the lot, I feel as if I've given myself a hernia.

Hopefully, when my doctor examines me, he will think my symptoms are sufficient to merit a handicap tag.

PARIS 3.0

I had been wanting to go back to Paris for a long time. I wrote about it in my last book. It's one of my favorite cities.

But when I looked back at the date of my last trip, I was shocked. My first trip there was in 1986 and my second was 1993. So I had last been there thirty years ago. "Time flies" is not just an expression, it's a fact. But finally, now, I was heading back to Paris.

I wondered if the city I had been so enchanted with as a young man would have the same appeal at sixty-one. Would I once again fall in love with Paris? Will it feel the same?

As we made our way to the airport, I couldn't believe how little preparation I had done. Other than get my clothes and toiletries together, and condense them into a couple of carry-on bags, I had done absolutely nothing. I hadn't looked online to see if there were any special exhibits or shows or concerts planned in the city. I hadn't checked for restaurant reviews or things close to my hotel. Nothing.

I used to be such a planner. But as I have aged I've noticed I'm definitely more relaxed about travel. And I must say I like that. I really like going somewhere with no set agenda, and just letting things unfold.

I was making the trip with Sarah. Her daughter, son-in-law, and granddaughter were planning to be there for the summer, so I figured I would just let them take the lead. I did have a list of three or four things I really wanted to do, things that had left a lasting impression on me from before. I had kept this list filed away in my brain for the last thirty years.

One was to re-visit the palace and grounds of Versailles, and another was to see Sacre Coeur again. But the main one was to repeat my late-evening walk up the Champs-Élysées, in the glow of all the beautiful Paris lights, making my way to the Arc de Triomphe. I vividly recall the arch being flooded with light, and all the trees along the way covered with twinkling lightbulbs. The avenue literally glowed. That walk was one of my favorite experiences from my first trip, or any trip, and I wanted to share it with my friends.

Beyond that wish list, I was pretty much wide open for new experiences. I often think the biggest mistake people make when traveling is going somewhere with the mindset that you'll never return. You end up in a mad dash to see everything—since this is seemingly your only shot—and end up not really enjoying or savoring anything.

I have certainly been guilty of this in the past. I still catch myself starting to worry about dinner plans, or possibly missing the train hours before I need to, but I try to return my eyes and ears to the moment at hand. It's human nature, I think, to get ahead of ourselves. But I'm trying to do less of that.

Sarah had never been to Paris but, as it turned out, both Sarah and I were in agreement about this trip. Of course we wanted to do some of the big things, the things long-associated with the city of Paris. But the main thing we wanted to do—that I had not done on my past trips—was to just explore and take in the city at our own pace. We both wanted to relax and really savor it.

I heard that a heatwave had hit Europe, but wasn't all that concerned. My hotel would have air-conditioning—I cannot sleep in a hot room—and I figured if I could get a good night's sleep, the rest would take care of itself. I figured we could just stay in the shade during the hottest parts of the day.

We arrived with our linen shirts in the middle of July and realized quickly that Paris was indeed experiencing a surge of high temperatures. It felt like Tennessee in August.

One thing that shocked me on this visit, though, was how much easier the language situation was.

Back in '93, the language barrier seemed a much bigger problem, as if the French either didn't speak or didn't want to speak English. I vividly remember some scowls and sneers when I would speak in English. I even heard a few giggles. I wasn't sure if it was because I was an American or Southern—or just ignorant—that they were so entertained. But whatever the reason, I definitely heard some laughs as I walked away from the counter at some of the bakeries and ice cream shops.

Perhaps it was because I was a typical American *tourist* on that first trip: I just expected people to speak English. I remember being excited, and nervous, and hurried. I had never been out of the country. I was trying to take it all in, and do that as quickly as possible. I doubt I was taking the proper time to engage the Parisians. I have since learned that they want to be greeted, and engaged, before jumping right in and speaking in English. But back then I didn't really care if some of them seemed rude—let them laugh, or eat cake, I thought. Paris was just too beautiful for me to worry about a few sneers.

But now, on this trip, I really didn't encounter anyone who wouldn't attempt to communicate in English. This time around, I tried to greet them in French, smile, and at least ask them if they spoke English before launching into my question, and this seemed to do the trick. Many times, if the staff heard us speaking English at our table, they would come over and greet us in English, which was very kind I thought. So, the language thing, which I had kind of dreaded, turned into a non-issue.

What did turn into a major issue was the heat.

I quickly realized I was totally unprepared for it. It was in the 90s every day, very sunny, and just plain hot. I somehow seemed to completely forget that all my workouts at home were indoors—in air-conditioned space. And, yes, at home I walked outside several times a week, but usually after the sun went down, so it was much cooler. Even though I thought I was in shape, mother nature let me know quickly that I was not—certainly not in shape enough for this Paris summer.

As much as I wanted the focus of this trip to be on the beauty of Paris, too often it was on my tired body. I was not only hot and sweating profusely, my foot was killing me, and I would have murdered any unsuspecting passerby for a glass of fresh-brewed iced tea.

(I really don't want to dwell on the negative—and it does seem like I spend a lot more time these days writing about aging and ailments—but I write what I know, and this seems to be what's happening in my life.)

My foot was definitely not cooperating on this trip. Before I left for Paris, I had been having some pretty noticeable pain, but I stupidly just dismissed it. I knew it was plantar fasciitis. I'd had it before and it always went away with some stretching and rest. So I just left it to take care of itself.

Big mistake. The hotter it got and the more we walked, the more my foot hurt and the more I would sweat. I was not a pretty sight. I felt every single day of my sixty-one years.

I still loved everything we were seeing and doing, but limping your way around Paris is not ideal.

I so wanted this to be a trip that allowed me to appreciate all the aspects of Paris I had been too rushed to experience on my first two visits. I wanted to roam, to stroll, to stop at cafés, to stand on the bridges and look out at the water, to really *see* Paris and let it soak in. And for the most part I did, I just hadn't planned to do it with a limp.

I had also not accounted for my addiction to iced tea.

I have very few vices. I don't smoke, drink alcohol, do drugs or even drink coffee. But I do need some iced tea daily. It's relaxing, refreshing, and it gives my brain a much-needed jolt of caffeine. This is my one little vice. Can't I at least have this one?

I had hoped that since there were Starbucks and McDonalds in Paris, that I might be able to find some actual brewed iced tea at one of those American chains. This was another big miscalculation. Every place I went in Paris had something they called iced tea—but it was not. It was some kind of Lipton peach tea that tasted awful, full of artificial sweeteners. I looked everywhere for a real glass of iced tea. The menus all listed iced tea, but each and every time it was that disgusting fake peach tea. After the third day I quit asking.

I hadn't ordered a Coca Cola in decades, but I ended up turning to them every day for my hit of caffeine. I had more Cokes in a week in Paris than I had drunk in the last twenty years. In the grand scheme of things, I guess that's a small sacrifice for a week in Paris, but I did file a note away in my brain. *Cannot ever move to Paris—no iced tea.*

Here's another thing that confounded me: eating.

I like to eat. I like to eat breakfast. Especially when I am going to be walking all day. I need a breakfast with some protein. I need more than a croissant and a cup of coffee.

Obviously, no one else in Paris did. Most of them didn't even need the pastry. People were everywhere, sitting in cafés having a cup of coffee and maybe a smoke for breakfast. Enjoying each other's company, but not any food.

I don't get it. How do they function? Don't they know that breakfast is the most important meal of the day? If they had grown up in America, they would. I like to eat a good breakfast with eggs and maybe some grits or potatoes and, of course, toast. After my first couple of days there—having just a pastry for breakfast—I quickly realized that this absolutely would not work.

I looked for a charming Parisian café offering anything other than coffee and a pastry and could not find one. So I stopped in the McDonald's right by my hotel for an Egg McMuffin. I didn't want to eat at McDonald's in Paris. It seemed wrong. But I will admit that, to my stomach, that Egg McMuffin felt oh-so right.

On about the fifth day, I found a café not too far from my hotel that actually had eggs on the menu. I was so excited. I couldn't wait to go there the next morning. They had scrambled eggs and omelets. It seemed like a dream—too good to be true.

I thought it would be crowded since this seemed to be the only place in Paris that served a real breakfast, but no, I was wrong. There were maybe four people there, all drinking coffee. I think one was eating a croissant. I guess this explains why they are all thin. I took a seat at the back of the café, and was told if I wanted eggs I had to order the full breakfast.

Hell yes to that.

I ordered the first full breakfast option from the menu (there were two). It included an omelet, bacon, bread and jelly, hot tea and a small juice. That seemed more of a modest breakfast to me. Usually where I eat at home you get a side of potatoes with that.

Apparently, they always bring a croissant when you order anything, so with the croissant, and the rest of my breakfast, my small café table was quite full of plates and cups. When the waiter left, I once again scanned the room to see if anyone else was eating anything.

Nothing.

No one was eating but me.

It wasn't difficult to observe that I had more food on my table than everyone in the restaurant combined, including the patrons out on the sidewalk. I supposed I looked exactly like the typical, gluttonous American tourist that people in other countries talk about.

I didn't care. I just smiled to myself and ate every bite of food on the table and drank my hot tea and juice.

It wasn't the best I've ever had, but it was the best I had there, and I loved it. Let them think I am a typical American tourist stuffing my face. Who cares? The sad fact was that even though it appeared I had eaten a huge amount, this wasn't as much as I would usually eat at home on a Saturday morning. I decided not to share that with the waiter. I was already getting more than enough attention. At least I didn't lick the plates.

I went back the next day and I ordered breakfast number two with the scrambled eggs. I had at least solved the breakfast problem.

Throughout the week, I had been telling my friends about the amazing lights along the Champs-Élysées, and how beautiful it was at night. I had really built it up. Since it didn't get dark there until around ten in the evening, we had decided to wait until the last night to take that in.

I thought this would be a nice little climax at the end of our trip. I had been so exhausted after all the walking and sight-seeing on the previous days that I would be in bed by 10 p.m. So on this last evening, sure I was tired, but so excited to see the Paris lights. We went to dinner late, took our time, and walked what seemed like a long, long way toward the Champs-Élysées.

By this time, late in the trip and late in the evening, I was limping, literally dragging my foot at times. I was miserable, but damn, I wanted to see those lights again.

When we finally got there, it was close to 10 p.m. and something seemed very wrong. I couldn't see any lights. It wasn't completely dark yet, so I thought maybe the lights hadn't clicked on. We walked some more, but things looked nothing like I remembered. It wasn't nearly as charming. The cafés didn't seem as inviting and neither did the shops. We waited, and we waited, but no lights.

Finally, I looked it up on my phone. What time do the lights come on?

They don't. THEY DON'T.

Wonk. Wonk. Wonk.

I could hear those horns in my head as I read the article. Wonk. Wonk. Wonk. This felt exactly like Chevy Chase arriving at Wally World to find it closed for repairs.

According to the article, a few years ago they turned off the lights to conserve energy.

Well, shit.

I continued to read and found out they now only turn on the lights for certain holidays. So for most of the year the magnificent Arc de Triomphe is not even lit.

Now that is just wrong. I'm sorry, but someone needs to cough up some tax dollars. This needs to be illuminated every day—damn the cost. It's one of the great symbols of the city. The Eiffel Tower was lit up like a Christmas tree so why not this arch? I was so disappointed.

My friends were all tired and not nearly as disappointed as I was because they hadn't seen what I had seen years ago. I even found a photo on my phone to show them what they were missing, but they still didn't get it.

I was pissed off and wanted to go on a rant like Chevy Chase and demand they turn the lights on. I had traveled from afar—like the wise men. But I was simply too tired to create a scene. I was a little humiliated too, since I had spent so much time hyping the lights without checking the schedule. But who would think to do that?

I could not have realized then, looking at the dark arch, only visible in the shadows, that this was not my biggest humiliation of the trip. It was still to come.

We made our way to the train for our last ride in Paris, heading back to the hotel. I was so tired, and my foot, well, by now, it was throbbing. I was trying to act like it didn't bother me, but the sweat on my forehead, and the limp I had gained during the week, probably gave me away.

I followed Sarah, her daughter and granddaughter onto the train. I sort of stumbled a little bit, but I grabbed the pole for stability. The metro was terribly crowded all during our trip. But I was quite surprised by how polite the French were during our rides. Every time we boarded, without fail, some young man would get up and offer his seat to Sarah. I was impressed. There were very few times any seats were available, so I never even tried to get one. Some days I would have really loved one, but I never let on.

I stood there frustrated by my foot, and hating that I was covered in sweat because I wasn't in the best of shape. This is not the look I wanted to convey. And as hard as I tried to convince myself otherwise, I knew I wasn't fooling anyone. I felt like an old man.

The final blow came on that last train ride in Paris. Sarah had been offered a seat, which she took, but Sarah is eighteen years older than I am, so that's ok. If I were seventy-nine, I'd take a seat too. But I was way too young for that I thought. Surely these people could see that.

But no, they didn't.

A nice young man got up and offered me his seat.

I was about to extend my hand and brush away his nice gesture. I wanted to let him know that I had no need for a seat. But as I did, a week's worth of exhaustion hit me like a ton of bricks. The hand that was supposed to brush him away instead took the rail where he had sat.

Humiliated, defeated and embarrassed, I took the seat.

I sat down. And it felt good.

I hated how good it felt. The young man in my head couldn't believe I took the seat, and the old man in my head thought hallelujah-and-praise-the-lord for this piece of plastic that was now supporting my tired old ass.

On that last train ride in Paris, I thought, damn, it has come to this. I look so old that I am being offered seats on the train. What's next, a wheelchair at the airport?

I left Paris in a quandary. Yes, Paris, you are a beauty, but a harsh mistress indeed. Your architecture is stunning beyond compare. The people are stylish and the scenery is breathtaking.

But not a drop of fresh-brewed iced tea to be found anywhere, and I've never felt so old. I guess that's a sacrifice I'll make for the rest.

On the way to the airport, I started thinking about the differences between Paris this time and Paris when I was there the first time over thirty years ago. It took a few minutes to sink in. Paris really wasn't all that different. Sure, everyone has a cell phone now, but what was most different this time was me.

That first trip, I was obsessed with doing all the big things. Seeing all the landmarks that the city is known for. And you need to do that. They are all worth seeing. And I did that.

This time was more about the little things. The stuff in between the big things. The stuff you miss when you are running from the Eiffel Tower to the Lourve to look at the Mona Lisa before they close. Things that really resonated with me this time were small things, like the little marketplace full of artists in Montmartre, up on a high hill in Paris, surrounded by the most charming cafés. I also remember all the beautiful homes and chateaus along the steep sidewalks as we made our way down from that high plateau.

I remember the ingenious way one café owner cut

off the front legs of the bar stools so that he could squeeze-in more patrons on the crowded sidewalk. I figured there was some city ordinance that all the stools had to fit on the sidewalk, and his did—barely. The front legs of the stools still sat on the sidewalk and the rear, longer legs, sat down in the gutter. You had to be careful if you took one of those stools.

I so enjoyed the space and beauty of the Picasso Museum. On my other trips, we tried to enjoy the Lourve, but the vastness and the crowds made that feel overwhelming. This small, beautifully done museum was a perfect way to enjoy this artist, and was quite fulfilling.

And this time I was blown away by the number of people traveling around the city on bicycles, and the speed at which they moved. I was impressed by all of the pedestrians—not one carrying their drink. They don't do that. They sit at the cafés and savor their coffee. I loved seeing that. It seems that at home, we can't run out the door fast enough, spilling half our coffee on the way. They are wired differently.

I won't forget hundreds and hundreds of cafés and shops and churches all over the city, or the train rides, or the gardens, or the apartment buildings—each covered in Paris stone.

Yes, this time it was definitely the little stuff—the stuff in-between the big stuff—that I'll remember. And I'll cherish the time spent with friends in that great city, the city they—ironically—call the City of Light.

I hope it's not thirty years before I visit again. But when I do, I'll know to call ahead, and tell somebody to flip the damn switch.

A Day at the Beach

I haven't been to the beach in a long time, but that's by choice. It seems that most people yearn for the beach. They long to be "at one" with the ocean, and feel the sand between their toes. They cannot wait to pack their tote, don their swimsuit and take off —carefree—for a day by the ocean. They count down the days until they arrive at this place they love, this place that is the most relaxing haven they can imagine.

Isn't it amazing how different we all are?

Things that some people find so enjoyable can seem almost painful to others.

For example, a Disney vacation? Nothing about it appeals to me. The crowds, the lines, and the heat are bad enough, but the cuteness and required happiness are the ultimate turn-offs to me. And yet, I have so many friends who cannot wait to get there, and go often.

Not me.

And a day at the beach—for me—is much the same. I hesitate to use the word *torture*, but the experience comes pretty close in my mind. The stress

A Day at the Beach

I feel even *preparing* for that day is more than enough to keep me at home. Trust me, I would never make the decision to go spend a day on the beach of my own volition. But, when I am talked into going, I look forward to it with as much enthusiasm as a root canal.

See, since I am really pale and burn very easily, I have to spend a good bit of time prepping my skin. I don't think other people have to go through this much crap. When I used to go on Caribbean cruises, I would use a tanning bed and try to build up a tan in order to avoid bad burns from all the sun exposure. I know this is not a good solution to the problem, but I always heard that it's better to build up a tan gradually than to get a sunburn.

While I am sure there is some truth to this, for me the process is a nightmare. I have to go to the tanning salon weeks in advance of the trip, start off with five minutes in the bed, and then move up to seven minutes, and so on. It takes at least five or six visits before I see any sort of color, and it takes a good three weeks for me to get even a slight tan.

It's a royal pain in the ass. I don't fit in most of the beds either, and then I don't tan evenly. I usually would end up somewhere between pink and a very light tan. It wasn't ever pretty.

The only good thing is that, by doing all this preparation, I noticed that I didn't burn when I was exposed to the sun on my trip. This is probably because I had slowly microwaved myself in the tanning oven and fried my internal organs in the process.

I've only done this painstaking preparation three or four times—for some winter cruises—and have

A Day at the Beach

pretty much decided I will never do it again. It just seems unnatural to me, in the dead of winter, to go into a little room, strip down to your underwear, slather some sort of oil on your body, and broil yourself in a little torpedo-shaped oven.

When I choose not to go this route, I am left at the mercy of self-tanners for my day at the beach because I choose not to look like Casper The Friendly Ghost, and be sniggered at. Self-tanners also require several days of preparation and then I never have a good result. I still don't want to be seen in shorts or without a shirt because I feel that my tan is fake-looking, or too orange, or uneven. And then of course, I don't have an actual tan, so I have to use lots of sunscreen for protection from sunburns.

Then there is the packing for this day of fun. You need a swimsuit, some sort of shoes or flip-flops, a shirt, hat, sunglasses, sunscreen, and towels. You are also going to need food and drink, a book, your EarPods, phone, a beach chair, and maybe some beach toys like a frisbee or some blow-up beach balls. I literally moved into my first dorm room with less stuff than this.

But let's for a moment assume that I have done all this preparation and packing, and have made my way to the beach. And let's also say that some nice person in my group has gotten up early and gone down to the beach, rented an umbrella and reserved some chairs. In this case, at least I have a place to sit. (I sure as hell would never do this myself, but we are suspending reality for a moment.)

So here I am, actually on the beach.

I have placed my towel over my chair and now I

am reclining with a book. Let's also assume that we have a decent view of the ocean. But before I can enjoy this view, I have to put on my first coating of sunscreen. I will agree that the ocean is pretty to look at and relaxing to be near, and for a brief moment I actually enjoy myself. Within a few minutes though, the heat causes me to sweat and the sunscreen begins to run into my eyes and they are burning, so I have to find my eye drops. Thank God I brought them to the beach along with everything else I traveled to Florida with.

Heat is a big part of a day at the beach. I might be currently under the umbrella but, as the sun shifts during the day, I have to move either myself or the umbrella to keep myself out of the sun. *I can handle this* I think to myself. *I will be fine. I must enjoy myself.*

So now it's been a while and I'm feeling warm and decide to stroll down to the water's edge and dip into the ocean. But first, I have to hide my phone and EarPods and secure everything at my location.

Then I take a stroll, noting along the way that even with all my preparation, I look like a ghost compared to all the regular beach people. But I do walk into the ocean, trying not to step on shells, or crabs, or jellyfish, or the obnoxious little child that always seems to find me, wanting to be my friend because I am the tallest person he has ever seen. And yes, the water is cooling, and yes, once again, I temporarily enjoy myself.

After some splashing around and feeling a wave or two assault me, I make my way back to my chair and read a little while. And after what seems like hours, I look at the time and realize that I have now been at the beach for a full...forty-five minutes. I am exasperated at the thought that I have at least four or five hours left to "enjoy."

During all this time that I am supposed to be experiencing relaxation and pleasure, I find myself drinking lots of water because the temperature is rising and the sun is now baking me. I realize I need to go pee, but I'm at the beach and the nearest restroom is about a mile away. So I secure my belongings again and set out for a nice walk in the blazing sun. As I make my way through a crowd that has accumulated around me, I cannot help but notice all the other beach-goers laying totally zoned-out in their beach chairs or on their towels, all tan and napping contently.

They are definitely pros at this and I am obviously a total amateur.

And once again it hits me. The beach has won. I have lost. I simply cannot figure out how to do it.

Is this something I would like to be a pro at? No. I don't have the skin for it. Nor do I have the mental capacity for it. I think you have to be able to unwind, and relax, for hours at a time, and that's something that I am simply not capable of.

Maybe an hour of relaxation is something I can do. Maybe even two. But please don't ask me to enjoy myself for a full day.

I've tried to do it many times over the years, on various trips, and it always ends the same way. A day at the beach is some of the hardest work I've ever done. I've watched in amazement at my travel companions as they soak up the sun and the beach without a care in the world. I sit there, wide-awake, looking at them and thinking *what is wrong with me?*

So, after a couple of hours, feeling totally defeated, I pack up my tote and head back to the hotel. Then I change into some street clothes and my walking shoes and head out for some sight-seeing—something I actually find enjoyable.

I might return to the beach in the evening for a walk along the shore at dusk. That's when I like the beach. At that time of day, I do find the ocean relaxing. By then most of the people are gone, it's less busy, and the ocean really does look peaceful and calm.

But a *day* at the beach? No way.

TOUR OF HOMES

Houses talk to me, at least some of them do. Some of them say, "Welcome in" and make me feel right at home. Others scream, "Help me!" begging to be rescued from horrible '70s renovations and foul shag carpeting.

I like that—the talking part, not the shag carpeting.

I love touring homes of all kinds: homes in terrible shape that are in need of help, or homes in perfect shape full of great design. There is always something to be learned or something to stretch my creativity. I like to roam around and let the house tell me what it needs.

Actually, this tendency I have applies to most any space I enter. I often become very distracted by the possibilities I see inside a space. Sometimes the possibilities are so distracting I can hardly concentrate on the conversation I'm having with my friends. I can usually turn it off, but if the space has lots of potential, I can only turn it down to simmer.

I've worked on a lot of houses—a whole lot. I've redecorated, redesigned, added-on, flipped, built-from-scratch, and everything in between. And, to be perfectly honest, I've loved every minute of it.

I really enjoy a challenge and some houses present great challenges. I love to buy the ugliest house on the street and give it a new lease on life. When I can solve problems with traffic flow and organization, and create more functional work and living spaces—all while making the house beautiful—then I feel like I have solved the Sunday Times Crossword puzzle.

Actually I cannot solve the Sunday Times Crossword puzzle. But I think I know what it would feel like, and to me it feels like taking a house with lots of problems and making it work—beautifully. That's what I like to do. That's my fun—better than snow skiing, or a hike in the mountains, or boating on the lake.

Doing this for so many years, I have learned to read the owners too. I can often look at the homeowner and tell, just by some things they say and the way they are dressed, what the inside of their house will look like. It's not always accurate, but many times it is.

Of course, it's pretty easy to take a look at someone and surmise that they have wind-chimes, dream-catchers and a hammock at home. That's kid stuff.

But I'm a pro at this. One time, I went to meet a lady about an addition to her home. I walked in and knew immediately that somewhere in that house was a portrait of Elvis, painted on black velvet.

I was right.

It's a gift. I try to use it sparingly.

This same woman, an older sort of disheveled-looking lady, said she kept a chainsaw handy and had no problem taking out a wall if it happened to block her view. At first I thought she was joking, but then I saw a single two-by-four propping up the ceiling between her kitchen and den. There were jagged shards of sheetrock hanging down where something had eaten its way through.

She caught me staring at the mess and explained that she was tired of not having enough light in her kitchen and went after the wall with her chainsaw. I was impressed—and, from the bowed look of that strained two-by-four, also terrified that the house would cave in on me at any moment.

While I often get a good sense about what people have in their homes from their personal style, sometimes I have absolutely no idea. Some people's home style is a polar opposite from their personal style, which really confuses me.

This well-dressed lawyer moved to Boonetown and opened up a new practice. He started out by remodeling this nice older brick home, turning it into a new office for himself. But—as my friend Maggie often says—someone needed to take away his credit cards.

I know everyone doesn't agree on what is stylish or attractive, but I think everyone did agree about this project. It was horrible. He took a perfectly attractive house and turned it into a complete eyesore.

But he wasn't finished.

Next he bought a beautiful old home. It was one of the few nice, large, craftsman-style homes in Boonetown. He did another, more-extensive renovation to this poor unsuspecting home. He added a couple more floors to the home, and the only way I can describe it is that it looks like a Swiss chalet landed on the roof and got stuck there. It was so bad that the Tennessee Main Street Association used photos of it in their "what not to do" slideshow.

This house happened to be on a Boonetown home tour one year, and I decided to go through it. It was equally bizarre-looking from the inside. And it felt quite unstable too. I think he had removed one too many support beams. I didn't linger very long. Now, decades later, we all still have to look at it. To me it's an eyesore. Indeed, someone should have taken those credit cards.

But sometimes it's the little things about people's homes that puzzle me the most. I was touring this prospective client's home and I noticed that there were no pillows on the beds. No decorative pillows, no shams, no sleeping pillows, nothing. The bedspread was covering the beds completely, like a tablecloth on a dining table. After seeing this in two or three bedrooms, I had to ask about their pillows. I said, "Do you keep your pillows in the closet?"

She looked at me like I was asking something absurd and said, "We don't use any pillows."

I said, "Not even to sleep on?"

Then she looked irritated and said, "No."

And she didn't offer an explanation. What chutzpah. I wish I could do that. Just say no and leave it at that. But I always end up giving a detailed summation of my reasoning.

I couldn't get it out of my head—the pillow thing. I was now hoping I didn't get this job because I didn't think I could decorate an entire house without using any pillows. It's not possible, I thought. What would

I put on the beds? And then I started wondering about their kids. Do they use pillows? If they have a friend sleep over, do they warn the other parents to send pillows with their children? Or do they just let them go home with a neck cramp?

I really do love touring homes, though. Real, lived-in homes. I love it when a home bridges that gap between great-style and lived-in. That's hard to accomplish for sure. There are some homes that do manage both, though. In those situations, I usually find that the homeowner has great personal style too. I like to be around those people.

One of these people was Winnie, a lady that I got to know through my parents in Boonetown. She was probably about sixty-five when I met her, and her hair was always kept in a sleek, silver-gray bob.

Her wardrobe was classic. If it was winter, she might be wearing her red-and-gray plaid Pendleton jacket with a gray turtleneck sweater and matching gray slacks. If the occasion was dressier, she was in her light-grey Ultrasuede suit. If it was warmer weather, she would be wearing a crisp, white blouse and cotton slacks. She didn't have many clothes at all, but she was always dressed appropriately and stylishly.

Her home was fantastic. On the exterior, it was a basic colonial-style home. On the inside, it had good bones, beautiful woodwork, and lots of character. It had a center hall that went from the front to the back of the house. (I later used that design feature in the house I built for myself.) She had many lovely antiques, lots of classic wallpaper, oriental rugs, linen drapes and a sunporch full of vintage wicker. So many of the things she had in her home in the '70s, are the things people are trying to put in their homes today. It had style and warmth and it definitely made an impression on me.

Winnie herself was quite a character. She was always smoking a cigarette. And in the evenings, after a cocktail or two, she would call me from her favorite chair on the sunporch. We would talk about our homes and antiques and whatever else might come up. She had redone her old home in Boonetown long before it was popular, and she was doing vintage when vintage was not yet cool.

In my mind, Winnie and that house will always be linked. She loved it so much, and it was a part of her. Being in that house felt like spending time with a good friend.

I've toured so many homes over the years. Lots of them were on the spring tour of homes in Savannah. For over a decade, I would plan a spring trip around their tour dates. These are homes with great architectural features and many of them are extraordinarily well decorated. So it's a great place to do tours. I've done a lot of the historic home tours there too, but they feel more like museums than real homes and I really don't enjoy those as much.

A lot of the homeowners in Savannah seem to have made no real preparation for the tours. They were too cool for that, too laid back. They didn't appear to have done any deep cleaning or a great deal of primping. There would be worn upholstery here and there as well as a few stains on the rugs, like at Winnie's house. The homes are lived in and welcoming like hers. The kind of place you wanted to be invited to for dinner. I am sure it would be a good time.

I went on another home tour over in Montery quite a few years ago. This was a tour of homes in the Montery historic district. I know I just said that I love houses that looked lived-in and comfortable. But this house was well beyond that.

I'm not sure who asked this older couple to open their home for the tour, but I don't think they gave them enough information. The house was a cute little Victorian cottage with interesting architectural details on the exterior. But inside it was definitely not a show house.

It was basically like going to visit my grandma and grandpa. And yes, this grandma and grandpa were both seated in their recliners, in the living room, watching TV, as the tour was in progress. I really felt like I was intruding. They seemed confused. They were cordial enough, but I was beginning to believe that they woke up that very morning having no idea they were going to be on a tour of homes that day.

I looked over at Maggie, who was with me, and I know she was thinking the exact same thing. I thought maybe they both had Alzheimer's disease and just figured all their children and grandchildren had come for a visit on the same day.

I definitely had my suspicions that they had no clue their home was on a tour. And when I got to the bedroom, those suspicions were confirmed. Someone had made up their bed, but on the night stand I saw eleven Mylanta bottles, and many other assorted medication bottles.

After we left the house, I asked Maggie if she had seen the eleven Mylanta bottles and she said, "Yes, of course I did, but there were thirteen. You must have missed the two on the dresser." Dang, I did miss those.

I am ashamed to admit it now, but we both had indeed counted the Mylanta bottles.

I just have to believe if they had known they were going to be on a home tour that day, and that hundreds of people would be walking through their bedroom, that they—or someone—would have put away those Mylanta bottles.

But, on the other hand, maybe they were far ahead of me. Maybe they were making an avant-garde home décor statement. Like the artists that somehow have their painting of a big red dot end up in a museum of modern art. These artists are too hip to paint a landscape or something identifiable, so they just splatter a big red dot on a white canvas and call it a day.

Maybe this couple was just really cool, too. They might have been making a political statement. Saying to the world, "This is real life. This is how we live. We don't subscribe to your decorator home tour expectations." And just to put an exclamation point at the end of their statement, they had been saving their Mylanta bottles for months.

Yes, they could have been doing that.

They might have been home-décor innovators.

But my money is on Alzheimer's.

The Green Café

I was in Savannah—my happy place. It was my last day there, and my friend John and I were looking for a place to have a quick lunch. Something simple is all we wanted. There are so many wonderful restaurants there but we had a flight to catch, so we just wanted to grab a sandwich.

Online I found this interesting-looking little café that wasn't too far from our hotel, so we decided to take a walk over and give it a try. It had a very strange name: Fate Primrose. We had no idea what that was supposed to mean, but the menu looked good.

It was in the Victorian District, a part of Savannah with a lot of colorful houses. So it didn't surprise me when we got there that the little vintage corner-store building had been painted a light mint-green color with darker trim. There were tables outside on the sidewalk too.

On the inside we found the décor to be a strange combination of styles. It felt something like the inside of a treehouse...or maybe an old pirate ship. All the walls were covered in wooden boards, or wood shingles, and the booths were built-in, made from repurposed wood with odd angles and curves. Tables were perched up on little balconies with ladder-like stairs for access. At the back, there was an order counter, and behind that were shelves of homemade goodies, breads, cookies, jams and jellies.

I couldn't help but notice that behind the cash register there was an oddly placed, round hole in the wall. I wondered what it was for, but I didn't have to wonder for long.

When I looked out the back door, I could see a nice patio dining area. I thought it would be a nice place for us to eat. Even if odd, the place definitely did have a cozy vibe and I could imagine it would be a great place to meet a friend for coffee or tea on a cold afternoon.

As soon as I walked in, I had a strong sense of déjà vu. I felt like I had been in the place, or somewhere similar, before. I knew I had not, so I kind of brushed that off and sat down for lunch with my friend John on the patio.

We waited for our sandwiches in a shady spot with a few other diners. I'd say there were no more than eight customers total in the place while we were there. A couple left, and a few more came in, but it was never what I would call crowded or busy.

What I did find interesting, though, was that the staff seem to be plentiful. Considering the small number of customers, I thought it odd that there were staff members all over the place, sort of wandering around.

When we arrived, a short man with hair parted in the middle, small round glasses, and a small pony tail at the nape of his neck took our order. He then printed out a receipt, put it in a little metal capsule, and threw it at the hole in the wall. I could hear the echoing sound it created as it made its way to its final destination.

I assumed the final destination for the little metal tube containing our order was a room on the other side of that wall. But then I remembered that the wall behind the order counter—this wall with the hole in it—was the exterior wall of this little building. Then it occurred to me that that tube must connect this building to the house next-door. I began thinking that this must be a larger operation than I had originally assumed.

After we took our seats at the table on the patio, things really started to get weird.

There was a little gate on the side of the patio that connected to the house next-door, where I figured our receipt had landed. I was guessing that that's where the kitchen was.

During the time that we were waiting for our sandwiches, several women and men made entrances from that gate (I assume from the house next door) and walked onto the patio and into the little restaurant.

I could tell that they were all some sort of staff members because of the way they were dressed. What really struck me as odd was that, even though the staff all seemed to be carrying out some kind of task, they looked emotionless. Their gaze was straight ahead, and even though they were carrying various pots, pans, and coolers, they didn't seem to be paying much attention to what they were doing.

I noticed the man taking our order had seemed a

bit confused too, but I just thought maybe he was new there, or maybe he was just a tad stoned. I definitely got a "hippie" vibe from the place, so maybe that was it, maybe they were smoking pot next door. He had the same look on his face as what I saw on the faces of the other workers coming through that gate—dazed and confused.

They were all in an odd sort of uniform. At least all the women were. They had their hair in these short ponytails. The shirt was a smock-style top, like surgeons wear, except in floral print, and they all wore these loose, flow-y pants, in burgundy or dark blue. The pants were gathered with elastic at the ankles. It took me back to the old *I Dream of Jeannie* television show. These were a more modest version of the harem pants that Jeannie wore, but they were definitely a type of harem pants—though these ladies weren't showing any of their midriff. I think some rappers also wore these pants in the '90s, but I can't recall which rappers. Whatever they were called— these shirts and pants—they looked equally weird on all the women, from the teenagers to the great-grandma. ("Great Grandma" had broken the hair code with a long gray braid down her back, but I bet it was grandfathered in.)

As we were eating lunch, I told John about this place near Boonetown, over in Monterey. I had been there for lunch only once. I remember it well, because it definitely had the same kind of vibe to it. This was a good fifteen years ago and I was there with my good friend Brenda. Don't ask me why, but for some reason we had stopped in for lunch.

We had heard rumors that this café was run by some kind of religious cult, but we had also heard the food was really good, so we thought it was worth a shot. It was called the Green Café and it was painted a similar shade of green to the building we were in now. I kept thinking what a strange coincidence this all was, since I was once again dining in a crazy, green luncheonette.

When Brenda and I sat down at the Green Café in Monterey, someone brought us some type of special "tea" to try even before we were given a menu. Brenda told me there was no way she was drinking any of their "special tea" since she had no idea what was in it. I kind of felt the same way.

After all, we were old enough to remember when Jim Jones had all his followers drink the poisoned Kool-Aid, killing them all instantly. If there was one thing we had learned, it was to never drink the Kool-Aid when visiting a new cult. When the waitress left the table, Brenda threw her Kool-Aid in the potted plant next to our table. She said, "Let's see if this thing is still standing when we leave."

As we ate our dinner at the Green Café, just like at Fate Primrose, we noticed there were many more staff members than customers. We also noticed they were walking back and forth from the restaurant to a house next door—with the same dazed and confused, straight-ahead stare. We figured the house must be the living quarters for the cult. We didn't know if it was really a cult or not back then, but we figured these workers or devotees probably weren't sure if they were in a cult either.

I can't remember what the Green Café workers were wearing, it's been too long ago. But they definitely weren't average street clothes of the day.

They also had some type of odd uniform on, and they all had sort of an Amish-yet-Hippie vibe. It was just so strange. We felt sure it really was some kind of religious cult, just like we had been told.

Brenda and I both enjoyed our food—actually, it was delicious—but we never went back. That's how weird it was. I've never been one to pass by a good restaurant, but I feared the Kool-Aid too much to partake of the food a second time.

The Green Café is still there, though, and quite popular. I've always wondered if others thought it was normal or strange. I had done some research online and found that the Green Café was indeed run by a religious group and all the members signed over all their possessions when they joined. That explained a lot. There obviously was some kind of communal living situation as well, since they all moved back and forth between this restaurant and the house next door. In their foggy, dazed state.

As I told my friend John this, sitting there in Fate Primrose, I just kept thinking there were so many coincidences. But the two places had different names. Maybe this was another group all together. Maybe I was just imagining things. But by the end of the meal, even John had to admit it felt like some sort of a cult situation.

Before we headed out, John wanted to get a loaf of banana bread to take home, and I waited outside. I was busy watching the activity at the house next door to our lunch spot. When he came outside after paying for his bread, he handed me a brochure he had seen on the counter. On the cover it said, "All the places you can find a Green Café."

Damn. YES. I was right. It did have some connection with the Green Café back in Monterey.

Inside the brochure were all the locations of Green Café's, and they were all over the country. I had no idea. I just thought there was that one near Boonetown. This was a much bigger deal than I ever imagined. Apparently, some of them went by the name Fate Primrose, like the one here in Savannah, but they were all part of the Green Café organization.

I love it when I'm right.

As we headed out, I looked back at the house next door. It was indeed where my order had landed after the man threw it through the hole in the wall. I imagine that kitchen served the restaurant and was also where the food for all the member-residents was prepared. This would explain all the large pots and pans the workers had been carrying around.

The house wasn't very large. I can't imagine it could house all the people I had seen working there, even if they had bunk beds lining the walls. But real estate in Savannah is very pricey and I guess this is the best they could do. Or maybe there was satellite housing elsewhere.

It saddened me to see some young women there, on the front porch of that house, with a baby in a carriage, about to go for a walk. They might have been as happy as could be, but I couldn't think of anything much worse than living life in a communal religious cult. They looked empty, like they had no thoughts.

But then, I had a thought. I thought of a "something worse": living your whole life, every single day, in a floral smock and big, I-Dream-of-Jeannie, flowing, harem-pants. Yep, that would definitely be worse.

I wanted to rescue them. I thought to myself, if I could just convince them to leave, I would take them to Target and buy them some straight-legged trousers.

But I didn't know if they even wanted to be rescued. And, if there is anything I learned from watching the ending of the movie *Pretty Woman* way too many times, it's that you have to want to be rescued "right back."

Oh well, we had a plane to catch. We turned and headed back toward the hotel.

I couldn't help but fear I might suffer some effects from the "tea" I had with my sandwich. Since I was thirsty, I hadn't thought to throw my tea in the potted plant as Brenda had done back when we first discovered the Green Café so many years ago in Monterey. Perhaps a leg would go numb, or some temporary blindness might set in, I wasn't sure. But I was hoping for the best.

I thought of so many questions on the ride to the airport. Does the Green Café in Monterey now require all workers to wear a floral smock and harem pants too? Is there a hole in the wall—to throw your order through—at every location? Will John like the banana nut bread? Did that potted plant in Monterey survive the Kool-Aid?

One wonders, but I doubt I'll be back to check.

GIVING CARE

I was in Panera Bread one morning, sitting alone at a table. An eightyish-looking older man was sitting at a table with a fiftyish-looking woman, and they were having a labored conversation. I heard him ask her in a very low tone, "Am I in trouble?"

I wanted to cry. It's heartbreaking. My mind immediately jumped right back to all the times I've been the caregiver for an older person. I know that look so well. When a smart, talented, dignified person has once again become the child, now living in a much smaller world inside their mind.

Even worse is knowing that, sadly, this time they won't grow out of it.

They are depending on you for help with medicines and meals, for transportation, and they are so scared you might forget them. They want to be on their best behavior, seeking your approval, so you won't abandon them.

You wonder if they aware of their forgetfulness, or angry outbursts, or confusion. You wonder if they know that they are asking the same question over and over. You hope they don't realize they are in this situation. Their mind is a scrambled mess of memories and moments that they can no longer see clearly or even in the correct order. When you look in their eyes, you can see the former person in there somewhere. And you want so badly to free them.

You can only hope they will keep some kind of dignity until the end. You also can't help but pray for the same thing for yourself, because inevitably, if you live long enough, you'll end up right back where you started—helpless and in need of care.

When my dad suffered a massive heart attack—ironically while in the hospital visiting his brother—he was revived in the emergency room. They worked on him for over two hours, during which (we found out later) his heart stopped fourteen times. Each time he was shocked and brought back to life. I got to the hospital about forty-five minutes after the incident began but was never consulted by the attending doctors. I'm not sure what I would have done, but I think, after he died maybe ten times, I would have asked for them to leave him at peace. Because someone, somewhere was obviously saying that it was his time to go.

But they didn't ask me, and what remained was a person with severe brain damage. He no longer knew who he was, or who we were, and couldn't carry on a conversation. After several weeks of therapy—which he would not participate in—he was still unable to communicate. It was a sad ritual during each visit. I think he was aware that he didn't know things he should know, so he would try to act like he did. He acted like he recognized us—and he probably did on some level—but didn't know our names. When he did talk he rambled through strings of unrecognizable phrases—some from his youth, some from jobs, and some from who knows where. It was like the hard drive on his computer got damaged and he could no longer access the information properly. This wasn't dementia, but just as frustrating.

There were some days that he seemed a bit more like himself.

One of those days was when Alice came to visit him.

Alice was a lady-friend he spent time with after my mom had died. They would go out to dinner occasionally and that sort of thing. Alice adored dad and came to visit him often in the hospital. One day, she thought she would play the CD recorded during his days in the Sharp Notes singing group. He loved being in that group and loved singing. I happened to stop in that afternoon. She was playing the recording and was singing along with it, urging Dad to sing along as well.

After a couple of songs, she asked him if he was enjoying the sing-along. In a moment of clarity, and a return to his true personality, Dad said, "Well the music on the CD sounds good, but that singing you're doing sounds like shit." I tried not to laugh out loud, but this was the first glimmer of my dad we had seen in a week. The rest of the time, he just couldn't seem to bring himself to the surface.

This was the second time in a few years we felt like he might not survive.

A few years prior to this heart attack, when my mom was still alive—fighting ovarian cancer—he suddenly became ill with a severe attack of diverticulitis. I think the stress of dealing with her advancing illness brought on his attack. He resisted going to the hospital, since he wanted to stay with my mom. But after several hours it was obvious he had to go.

His colon had ruptured, and all that poison was leaking into his body. He was swollen and infected and very, very sick. We were told that he would not have survived had we waited much longer to get him to the hospital.

He had a major surgery, and he had more tubes coming out of him than I had ever seen in one person. My sister and I were his caregivers. As tough as he had always been, this took him down. Getting him up to walk or to go to the restroom was like wrestling an octopus. There were poles and machines and tubes that all had to be handled just right so that he could move. Movement was incredibly hard for him. He was exhausted and still very weak. But he fought hard to follow doctor's orders and get up and walk. It took every ounce of strength he could muster.

I did my best to help him, and the hospital staff did their part, but it was a long, slow recovery. He never was a hundred percent again.

When he finally made it home, we had a caregiver there, named Terry, that had been staying with my mom and helping while Dad was in the hospital. She was an amazing human with a deep well of compassion. We really liked her and immediately felt a huge sense of relief when she came into our lives. Not only did she give amazing care to my parents when she was there, she also found other caregivers and managed them when she was not there. She was everything you hope for when looking for someone to help take care of a loved one. I would still be the caregiver during doctor visits and at times when the paid caregivers were not there, but I was so thankful that we had them most of the time. My respect for them grew every day.

Both of my parents were home again, but they were both tired, battered, and broken. I had never seen them down like this before. They had always been so tough and so healthy. But not now.

It's a sad-but-true progression if you live long enough.

You start off in diapers, in a bed with rails and safety guards. And, as your mind and body deteriorate, you end up in another bed with safety guardrails. Even worse, as an adult it usually takes more than one person to change your diaper.

I know one thing for sure. I would never want my family members changing my diaper, or bathing me, or any of that. I know that some people want that — their family as caregivers — and demand that of their closest family members. I'll never understand that. I think a lot of times they just don't want to spend money for help.

But I knew that my parents didn't want their children doing those things for them. And I can assure you that is not the last memory I wanted of them either. I hope that if that day comes for me, my caregiver is a total stranger — with vision problems.

My parents died too young, but if there is anything good about dying young, it is that they missed out on those extended years in diapers and living in nursing homes. I've heard of and seen so many people spending years and years bed-ridden, in a nursing home, and I can't think of anything much worse. My dad did end up spending his last five weeks of life in a nursing home, but mercifully, that was all.

The staff in those places are probably the most under-paid and under-appreciated people in the world. They handle the worst of the worst situations. They clean up the messes, deal with anger, screaming, abuse and never complain—and never seem to lose their sense of humor or compassion.

How they can maintain any sort of optimism for life is pretty amazing to me. Knowing that none of their patients will get well or return to their regular lives, knowing that today is the best things are going to get, and that a decline is inevitable.

My dad wasn't easy for the staff—at all. After his heart attack, he was confused and somedays very agitated. This man that had always been a model patient, respectful of the medical staff and cooperative, had become the very opposite of all of those. It had become so bad that he had to be restrained in his bed to keep him from hurting himself. He stripped off any clothing as soon as the nurses got it on him. This was probably the worst thing of all, knowing what a modest man he was, and now finding him undressed half the time. The staff was always so kind though, they would laugh and call him Houdini, because he was able to free himself from any clothing and every type of restraint they used.

I had a very difficult time with him removing his clothes. I knew if he were himself, he would never in a million years allow anyone to see him like this. We had tried all different types of pajamas and even jumpsuits, but he still got out of them. The thing was, they all had the closures on the front. So one day I got an idea, and headed to the store.

I bought some pajama bottoms and some large t-shirts. I went home and sewed the pajama bottoms into the hem of the t-shirts creating a one-piece combination jumpsuit and pajama. I named them JumpJams. I cut an opening down the back of the shirt and put some ties there that he could not reach. When I returned to the nursing home with the prototype, all the nurses were interested. Apparently, this was a big problem with lots of patients.

Well, JumpJams worked. He couldn't figure out how to get them off. Sadly though, he about drove himself into a fit of mental distraction trying to claw his way out of them. I didn't know if I had done something good or not. The nurses said I should patent them and sell them to nursing homes, but I never did.

Dad went into a sharp decline not too long after that and passed away.

The pj's had become a non-issue. I sort of forgot about my invention during all the things that follow losing your last parent. Settling an estate and filing all the final papers become your focus.

Years later, my aunt was at the same nursing home. She was suffering from dementia, had fallen, broken a hip, and was in a final state of decline. Still they never gave up on her. They took her to therapy, and to the lunchroom for group activities. On my visit one day, I found her at a table in the activity room. They had brought a group in for refreshments and bingo. Nell and I were at our table, and there were about six or seven other residents at various tables around the room.

The staff members excitedly served everyone a drink and some cookies. After the refreshments were finished—and by finished I mean the patients pushing the cookies around on the plate or picked at them lightly with shaky hands—they moved on to a game of bingo.

I don't recall any of the patients showing any interest in the game of bingo, but the young staff member pressed on and began announcing the bingo game. Nell always said she never won at bingo when she lived in the assisted living facility, so I thought maybe this was her chance for redemption. This was a weak field of competitors for sure.

My aunt was staring ahead and barely answering my questions. So, I began helping her with her card, and we were covering a lot of squares. One or two of the other patients were sort of participating, pushing around some of the buttons on their squares, but to say that anyone was into the game would have been a vast overstatement. The rest were mainly looking into space or down at the table, occasionally glancing at their card. The staff members were trying hard to get everyone interested and to participate. I couldn't help but think about how many times they had called those numbers with no one caring or covering their squares.

But they tried. They tried to give those residents a fun afternoon. They tried to keep their minds and bodies active. What a tough, losing battle to fight daily, I thought. I admired them so much.

And then, the saddest thought of all hit me. *Why weren't there more patients in the room playing with us?* There had to be close to a hundred residents there.

Well, then it dawned on me that these six or seven were probably the ones in the best shape or even able to come to the activity room. The rest were probably confined to their beds, or even in worse mental shape. Sad indeed.

Well, Nell and I did win big that day. Simply put, we kicked butt. But it was a hollow victory. Winning in a group of semi-conscious seniors felt wrong. I think we got to bingo first every game, but I quit calling bingo because I felt so bad. Truth be told, there were no winners in the room that day.

I sometimes look around at my generation and those younger than myself, and I wonder what kind of games we will be playing in the nursing home. I think bingo might be passé by then. I think a lot of games will involve tattoos. Trying to remember why you got the tattoo in the first place might be one game. And trying to let the other residents guess what the tattoo is supposed to be—after fifty years of sagging and drooping—might be another fun game. That Madonna tattoo from 2010 might look more like Mother Teresa by 2060.

One time a friend and I were at a restaurant and we both noticed a woman with a large old-fashioned pistol tattooed above each breast. She was displaying them for all to see. My friend looked at me after we walked by and said, "Those will be rifles in the nursing home." I had a good laugh about that. Maybe she will have some good laughs, too, on down the road.

I hear the line, "Growing old ain't for sissies" a lot these days. And it's true, no doubt. But I'll tell you what really ain't for sissies: caring for those who are growing old. The caregivers of our world are truly angels walking among us.

I think all the caregivers—the nurses, and aides, and orderlies—should be given a "get-out-of-suffering-forever" card when they retire. They should be allowed to bypass all the pain and disease and leave the world gently. They have earned it as far as I'm concerned.

I don't think it works that way—but it should.

Hair's the Thing

I was in the Nashville Airport the other morning and I saw an aging rock star. This happens pretty often. A lot of older rock stars live in Nashville now. And even if they don't, they visit there often to play a gig, to write, or maybe record.

They aren't hard to pick out. Especially at 8 a.m. in the airport because they are usually dressed exactly like they were dressed the night before on the concert stage. Not surprisingly, a seventy-something-year-old man dressed in tight black ripped jeans, black Cuban-heeled boots, a tight black t-shirt, and a black, distressed, flowing duster jacket is not hard to pick out on a random Thursday morning in the Nashville airport.

The clothes, of course, are always a big hint, but if there is any doubt, the hair is the dead giveaway. I don't know why it is, but so many of these celebrities —especially ones with a sort of trademark hairstyle— think they have to keep that exact same hairstyle for the rest of their life.

For like fifty years or so. The exact same hair style.

I always think of the neck pain poor Crystal Gayle

must endure on a daily basis just to keep her ankle-length hair. I realize her floor-length hair was a big talking point. I remember when I was a freshman at UNA, seeing her live in concert swinging her hair back and forth as she sang the big hit "Don't It Make My Brown Eyes Blue" from the stage at Flowers Hall. Her trademark hair probably did help her gain some fame early in her career as a twenty-something-year-old, and we all discussed it a lot around the time of the concert.

But that was over forty years ago. This woman is seventy-three years old now and, as of this writing, she is still wearing her hair just a couple of inches above the floor. Can you imagine how long it takes to wash, or dry, or color this mane?

I'll say this, she is dedicated.

I have to wonder if the rates are higher at the assisted living facility—should you have floor-length hair.

Surely she doesn't think that her fans would forget her if her hair was, oh, say, two feet shorter? Are her fans that shallow? I don't think they are, and I can't imagine that she thinks they are either. So I just can't help but wonder, as I have many times over the years, why she keeps her very long hair. I guess she really loves it.

It's the men that fascinate me the most, though. They are the ones that stand out most in the airport. The ones in their seventies, still sporting rock-and-roll hair.

Maybe they think they have great hair, like Jon Bonjovi did early in his career. Maybe that's what they see in the mirror. But guys, please take note:

Bonjovi—who was known for his trademark long curly blonde locks—is in his sixties and wearing short hair these days. And, as far as I know, his career hasn't ended and his popularity is still high. I think cutting his hair helped much more than hurt his career. Now he can at least secure some acting jobs and look relatively normal in a rom-com.

Not so for Alice Cooper, or Steven Tyler, or those guys from Kiss. They have stayed locked into their hairstyles with conviction. I saw Steven Tyler at the Green Hills Mall in Nashville once and could pick him out of the crowd simply because of his hair. Alice Cooper is another one of the older rock stars I've seen in person at the airport, and I'm sorry but the hair is just not helping. In my humble opinion, it's adding a good ten or twenty years to his appearance. I guess he still does have a good amount of hair, but like for a lot of people close to eighty, it's a lot thinner. It also looks brittle, maybe from all the dye and products.

I was seated next to John Oates—of Hall and Oates fame—on a plane not too long ago, and it was more of the same. He had his hair dyed jet black, in the same style as at the height of his career, and I think it really ages him. I did *not* point this out to him. But it was my observation.

I find it funny. These guys act like they don't want to be recognized, and yet they are dressed in full rocker regalia with aging rockstar hair for a simple trip to the airport. Their appearance does nothing but draw attention. It's the same with the country stars. If they weren't wearing the cowboy boots and a big cowboy hat, no one would even notice them. Sometimes I think they are protesting a bit too much.

Hair's the Thing

The clothes are an easy fix though. They can change outfits at any time. It's the hair that fascinates me. I guess I am just jealous. I began losing my hair in my early twenties, and by my mid-thirties I was pretty much bald. On the top of my head, at least. I still have a lot of hair on the sides and the back of my head.

If there had been good hair transplants back then, when I was thirty-something, I would have probably had them done, so that now no one would ever know. But back then, the hair transplants they offered were pretty noticeable. At least to me they were. They kind of looked like they had been stitched to your head with a sewing machine. So I figured I would just pass on those.

The toupees back then were pretty awful too. Many of them were ill-fitting, and you could see up under them. My dad made no secret of his aversion to toupees. He loved to point out an obvious one and would often say, "Nothing will ever replace natural hair."

But the worst hair offenders have to be comb-overs. Desperate men grow the hair on one side of their head about a foot long, and then sort of wrap it over their bald scalp. They then glue it all down with paste and hairspray. It takes a lot of work for these men to look this bad, and they still have to stay far away from wind or water.

Fortunately, you don't see these as much nowadays.

But just the other night I saw a man at the theater, and I had to take a moment to study his head. This wasn't just any comb-over. He literally had grown out

Hair's the Thing

the hair behind his left ear long enough to wrap all the way around his head, and circle back over that same ear. I would have to say this was more of a hair-swirl than a comb-over. It was quite a feat of hair engineering.

Ironically, the more hair I lost on my head, the more hair popped up elsewhere. Suddenly my ears were sprouting hair as well as my nose. Oh, and my back too. That's the most cruel twist of all. I was trying my best to regrow the hair on my head—using Rogiane—while simultaneously trying to get rid of it in several new locations.

And while we are talking about hair, there is another question that I have. It's a great mystery to me. (Well, for that matter, the entire human body is a great mystery and an incredible wonder. The fact that we are all able to walk and breathe and exist is truly amazing.) But this hair follicle mystery just drives me nuts: how do hair follicles know when to stop growing?

The hair on my head—what's left of it—has to be cut every two or three weeks. It grows insanely fast, but the hair on my arms, and my legs, grows to about one-half inch in length and just stops. This wouldn't be so weird if it just stopped after growing that much, and then the follicles were stagnant for the rest of your life. But no, they are not. If you shave the hair on your arm for some reason, it will grow back out to that one-half-inch length and then stop growing again.

How does it know? It's puzzling.

And what about your eye lashes? How do they know to grow to about one-quarter-inch length and then stop? And yet my beard, just a few inches below those eye lashes will grow to infinity without ever stopping.

Things like this just make me wonder. You have to admit. It's odd.

There are so many options now for reversing hair loss though that I do have to admit I am tempted to try. I have some younger friends that are using glue-on hair. This seems to be relatively new, and I guess it is a good solution if you don't want to have actual hair transplants. It's basically a toupee or hairpiece that is glued directly to your scalp. They look really secure and you can swim and shower with them. They are much more realistic-looking than the old toupees, but I still find some of them quite noticeable.

Some guys go to great lengths to hide the fact that they are now sporting a glue-on hairpiece, thinking you can't tell. But since they know you just saw them six months ago with a bald head, I think they should realize the jig is up.

One of my friends who got new glue-on hair is just totally out with it. He told me he has to go have his hair re-glued every three weeks and I admire his honesty.

This sudden popularity of the glue-on hair reminds me of the time back in the '80s when a local hairstylist started doing weaves for men. This, again, was a form of a toupee, but it was somehow woven into your existing hair to make it semi-permanent. For a while it was a big thing in Boonetown. Just like that famous day on *Oprah*, when everybody got a car, this was Boonetown and everybody got a weave. Well, all the bald men anyway. Well, except me, and of course my dad.

Hair's the Thing

Suddenly, several of the bald men at church—formerly quite noticeably bald—were rocking full, thick heads of hair. And they acted as if no one noticed.

I had news for them. Everyone noticed.

These days, I am content just to keep my hair buzzed really short, and gray. Sure, I would love to have a full head of hair again. And I would probably grow it down to my shoulders if I could, but I can't. And, even though the new hair transplants are virtually unnoticeable and permanent—no re-gluing every three weeks—I've grown accustomed to my bald head. And everyone knows I'm bald so the transplants would really be obvious. And frankly being bald is just too easy. I can wash and dry my hair in a couple of minutes.

I know for a lot of people their hair is their thing—their trademark. And I'll admit I am envious when I see someone with a great head of hair.

But I'm glad I never had trademark hair. I was never a rocker, or country music star, or anyone else with memorable long hair, so now there is no pressure on me to maintain it.

It does make life easier, and I never have to worry about being recognized at the airport.

My Left Foot

My Left Foot. Wasn't that the name of a movie? I think so. But if I were writing a movie called *My Left Foot*, I can tell you in one word what the plot line would be.

Pain.

My left foot has been a source of great pain for the last year. It's relentless. Plantar fasciitis is the diagnosis. And I will warn you right now that, just like my left foot, you might find this story long and agonizing. So if you have a low tolerance for pain, I suggest you skip this one.

Earlier in this book, in the story about Paris, you might recall that while I was in that beautiful city my foot was really bothering me. If you have forgotten, that's ok too. You are about to get a refresher. My foot was bothering me to the point of limping. It was —at times—excruciating.

I don't know why I didn't do more research on plantar fasciitis before I went to Paris—or even while I was there. I might have found some treatment I could try in my hotel room for some temporary relief, but I didn't. I tried to stretch it out at night but that's about it, and it didn't help. So by the time I got back home, my foot was in terrible—and I mean terrible—shape.

This was a big deal. Walking is not only my exercise but my mental therapy as well. It keeps me grounded and keeps me from feeling anxious. I needed to get this resolved quickly. My sanity was at stake.

Right after I got back to Tennessee, one my friends told me that she had plantar fasciitis, and the only thing that gave her any relief was wearing a pair of Hoka shoes. She said after wearing them a few days, she was pain free. She could not sing their praises loud enough.

So, off I went to Fleet Feet and bought a pair of the ugliest shoes I have ever owned. Trust me, there were much uglier ones in the store, in pinks, and teal-blues, and rainbow colors too. I have never seen such a display of hideous, huge shoes. I opted for the solid gray ones, the most basic looking ones they had because my feet are big—size fifteen to be exact. These Hokas already look large, even in a small size. Looking down at my feet, I thought a pair of battleships had docked at my pants' hem. They had thick, wide soles that splayed out all around the shoe.

I wore them out of the store, and by the time I got home, I had almost wrecked three times. My shoe kept getting hung up between the gas pedal and the brake pedal and the floorboard—at one point almost causing me to drive into a Walgreens. And by "into", I mean through the front wall of the store when the shoe got hung-up on the accelerator. These shoes were so big that in China they would have been considered a duplex.

My Left Foot

Anyway, I wore them for a few days, and my foot hurt worse than ever. To the back of the closet they went. No relief. Well, yes, actually some relief. I was greatly relieved that these shoes did not help my foot. Having to wear those ugly shoes the rest of my life would have been a miserable trade-off for some comfort.

I was at my wit's end and decided to go to the doctor. So I made an appointment with a new podiatrist in Boonetown. When I got there, I had a strong feeling of déjà vu. (Déjà vu happens to me often these days. I think that's because I'm over sixty.)

It suddenly hit me that the podiatrist was in this same office as the doctor I saw years ago for a neck injury. I pulled something or did something wrong, and had tremendous neck pain after wallpapering my bathroom. I'm not sure which was worse, the neck injury or the new foot ailment.

Solving my neck-pain problem was not easy. The doctor ordered an MRI to get the full story about my injury. Something was pressing on a nerve, or some other *something*, that was causing the pain to run from my neck, down my arm, and make my arm go numb at times. It was so uncomfortable I couldn't sleep and couldn't get relief in any position. I was miserable.

I had never had an MRI before and I ended up having a panic attack in that diagnostic hell-hole.

It took forever because I couldn't lay still. Every time I moved the machine had to re-set. But my shoulder was hurting so bad I couldn't help but move. So that was a bust. Then they sent me to an "open MRI machine" but this was worse. I felt like I was being squished in a panini press.

After two failed attempts at an MRI, the doctor sent me to physical therapy. This was the best thing he could offer with no definitive test results. As it turned out, I finally got some relief. It took a good while, but I finally was pain-free, without any surgery or any more MRIs.

I often wonder what happened to that doctor. He was kind of an interesting character. He looked like he spent a lot of time at the gym — probably a lot of time in front of the mirrors too. Not long after he treated me, I heard he got into a fist fight, in the Walmart parking lot, with another man, over his baby-mama.

The next thing I know, he moved away.

I'm not sure if that's the reason he moved away — the fist fight I mean — but it is very hard to overcome a fist fight in the Walmart parking lot when you are a doctor, and live in a town the size of Boonetown. People remember it. They will remind you about it too.

But now, here I was in this same office, seeing a different doctor about my foot. As I filled out the paperwork, it occurred to me that I knew something about this doctor as well. (This is Boonetown remember. Everyone knows everyone.) He is the doctor that bought my mom and dad's old house when he moved to town. It didn't click till I got there that day.

After some X-rays and a consultation — thank God no MRI — he felt, as bad as symptoms were, that I needed a cortisone shot and some steroids. He said he wanted to throw everything at it that he could to try

My Left Foot

to get me back to normal. He also suggested some shoe insoles which I immediately ordered.

As he was preparing the cortisone shot, he kept telling me that a lot of people found them to be very painful, trying to brace me for the discomfort. I was way beyond that, though. I didn't care about the pain anymore. I needed help. I told him to fire away. Give me everything he had. Hell, give me two shots. I just wanted something to work.

I left there with high hopes.

I felt some relief over the next few days. And I was staying off my foot because I thought that's what I was supposed to do. After a while though, when the drugs wore off, and I started walking again, the pain returned. The more I walked on it, the worse it got. This was not going away quietly.

I called the doctor back and he said the best recommendation at this point would be physical therapy. So I signed up for physical therapy—again. I had had good luck with PT in the past, so I was hopeful.

Going to a PT in your hometown is just like going to a class reunion—every visit. Seems I'm not the only one aging. All my classmates, former co-workers, and church friends were too. Every visit I would see someone, or even a few people, that I knew. Each time, I would have to catch-up with folks in the waiting room before my session, and sometimes during my session. It was kind of annoying to be honest. But I was trying to be sweet—hoping for good karma.

But karma wasn't good. I wasn't getting much relief there either. Maybe some. But not enough. It was like taking a half-step forward during the session, but by the time the of next session, I was two steps back. And I was doing my homework, and all kinds of stretching and such at home.

I began to bring it up—my left foot—everywhere I went. I was desperate to get any suggestion that might work. I asked anyone and everyone I saw. Much to my surprise, I found that everyone of a certain age—and I do mean everyone—either has it or has had it. My friend Renee, who cuts my hair, called it "the devil". She had been suffering with it too, but never mentioned it until I brought it up. We commiserated, but I had no real cure to share. Neither did she.

When I went to the furniture store to shop for a client, my friend Monita, who works there, said that she had it too. She walks all day on concrete floors, so hers was chronic like mine had become. From then on, every time I visited the store, we had to compare symptoms. She said she had begun dressing from the feet up. She would find the most comfortable shoes, and then put an outfit together around the shoes. I totally understood. I had been doing the same thing.

At my office, one of my coworkers who had it the previous year told me that she ordered a foot brace to wear overnight, and it had helped a lot. Up for anything, I ordered two different ones that very day. This is a gizmo that looks kind of like a slingshot. It goes around your foot and your ankle, and then pulls your toes back toward your ankle as you sleep.

I was skeptical of this, but to my surprise, I did feel some relief from using it. I began wearing it nightly. At least now I wasn't waking up with the severe pain. It would still become painful later in the day as I walked more, but it was not hurting so much in the morning. A little progress? Maybe so.

My niece told me she had gotten dry needling for her plantar fasciitis pain, and that this got rid of her symptoms. Wow, I thought, I must try it. So a call was made, and I had a bunch of needles sticking out of my foot later that day.

Since I was trying anything and everything, I tried to keep good mental notes of what worked and what didn't. See, by this time, many people had heard about my plight, and were asking my opinion on all the treatments I had tried. In a way, I felt like Columbus. Exploring new treatments and reporting back to the old country, or in this case, the old friends.

My friends, who had all suffered with this pain, were leaning on me to find the cure. So I was trying hard, not just for me, but for all the sufferers. It seemed every dinner out, haircut, or meeting with friends began with a ten-minute update on our current symptoms, pain levels and treatments.

I cannot say definitively if dry needling—which looked the same as acupuncture to me—helped or not. I went several times. It definitely didn't make it worse, but I'm just not sure how much it actually helped. I started wearing the night-brace shortly before the dry needling, and I was getting some relief at that time, but I can't really say how much. Was it the brace or the needling or the combination? I'm just not sure.

I had already planned a trip to New York for the fall, and had no intention of missing it. I had tried all these treatments hoping to be cured before New York, but off I went to New York with my pain-filled foot along for the ride. On the flight, I was contemplating how I might try to make my pain manageable for the trip, but I still wanted to walk a lot in the city. That's my thing, walking around New York. I love it.

My plan became to take short walks until the pain started and then take a break. It worked fairly well for a day or two, but on the third day there it was hurting again—badly. That day, I was walking on the Upper West Side, one of my favorite areas to stroll. I had to stay close to my hotel for fear of my foot rebelling. But I love that area, so I just walked up and down the side streets near Central Park—taking my time and trying not to overdo it. After turning a certain corner, I noticed I was in was front of a classic New York shoe store named Tip Top Shoes.

I limped in.

A young man attempted to wait on me, but he offered no real advice or expertise. So I browsed a while, still hoping for a miracle. Out of the corner of my eye, I could see an older gentleman. It appeared he was waiting on three different customers at the same time. He would watch them walk, analyze their issues, and then suggest shoes to help correct their particular situation.

I was there for it—watching with great interest. I waited to get his attention, and then introduced myself and asked if he could help me. I found out that he was Melvin and, according to Melvin, he was a foot expert. He gave me a list of his credentials with all the confidence of a military commander.

I decided right then and there to place all my confidence in Melvin. I was worn out, and I just wanted someone to tell me what to do. Melvin was

My Left Foot

ready for the job. He enjoyed telling people what to do, I could sense it.

First, he ordered me to walk around the room while he studied me. He mumbled this and that about my pronating or something. Then he told me to take off my shoes. Just as I was pulling my foot out of my shoe, he said, "Wait, wait, you are doing it all wrong. Don't you know how to take off a shoe properly?"

Well, I thought I did, but I guess I was being lazy and didn't fully loosen the laces. He was not having it.

"You are killing the life of your shoes. This is how you do it," he said, and then demonstrated. I bowed my head and promised to do better in the future.

Then he measured both of my feet and studied my arches for a moment. By this time, I had given him all the background information about my foot and all the things I had tried, including in the Hokas from hell and a few other stories. He was serious and still intently studying my foot.

He got up slowly. Melvin was not a young man. He was probably close to seventy. He walked toward the back of the store, and when he got to the staircase he yelled down to someone in the basement to bring a size-fourteen, model something-or-other New Balance. I usually wear size fifteens, but Melvin told me I was wrong.

Keep in mind that while Melvin was waiting on me, he was also waiting on at least two other customers. This gave me even more confidence in my new foot consultant. Anyone with customers waiting all over the store must know something.

While he was waiting for my shoes to be brought

up, he stopped and consulted with another patient. I think she had been a long-time customer because they seemed to have the drill down. Then he proceeded to the other side of the store, talking to another lady who was still trying out some shoes he had brought her earlier.

Melvin was the man. And Tip Top shoes was the place.

The walls were covered with shelves of every brand and style of good-quality walking shoe I had ever heard of. Shoes went from floor to ceiling, and there were just as many for men as women. I'd never seen even close to this many shoes on display in one store.

When my shoes arrived on the sales floor, Melvin slipped away from one of the other customers and picked up some size fifteen inserts along the way. I'd have never put size fifteen inserts in a size fourteen shoe, but I had given over all control to Melvin and I asked no questions. The key, Melvin said was all in the insert and fitting the arch. He removed the New Balance insole and inserted the new ones in what seemed like one swift motion. He had obviously done this before. Then he told me to try it on.

But before I could hardly get my foot in the shoe, Melvin started yelling at me again, "No, no, no, you dumb son-of a-bitch, don't know how to put on a shoe, where have you been?"

Apparently, I had not been at shoe school. Actually, Melvin didn't say the dumb son-of-a-bitch part out loud, but I knew he was thinking it.

Melvin said, "Good gosh man, you have to slide your foot in the shoe, and then tap, tap, tap, your heel on the floor to seat your foot in the shoe before tying up the laces."

I was getting more nervous by the moment. Melvin was tough, and I felt like I was disappointing him in every way possible. But at the same time, I loved it. I loved his confidence. I felt I was in good hands. He had me walk around the store in the new hybrid shoes, and they felt pretty good. Not instant relief mind you, but better. The insoles my doctor had recommended were similar, but they were hard and stiff. I didn't get much relief from them. These felt a lot better, firm but flexible.

My foot was in terrible shape, and I knew that any small improvement was a big win. Melvin told me that I must wear these insoles in all my shoes. I needed the support, and they would eventually get better. And I haven't had on a pair of shoes without these insoles inside them since.

I have so many good-looking shoes that I can no longer wear because the insoles won't fit, or the shoes are too stiff. But this is the price you pay for relief. I ordered a few more of the insoles so I wouldn't have to constantly be switching them in and out of my few pairs of shoes that actually feel good.

Before I left, Melvin had me try some small cotton pads under the insoles to see if they helped. He believes in really tweaking things. (I wore those for a while, but found that the insoles alone in a really good pair of supportive sneakers seemed to be the most comfortable way to go.) He then handed me off to another lady to check out. Melvin was far too valuable to be running credit cards. I'd love to know how many shoes he sells in a day.

My Left Foot

After that trip, my foot began to slowly improve. I don't think the insoles alone did it. I do think that wearing the nighttime brace also helped a lot. And time. I think it just takes a long time, considering how bad I let my foot get.

Its one of those not-so-rare conditions that everyone seems to have, and yet no one seems to have an answer for. Funny, until I started talking about it, I had no idea so many were suffering in silence. I feel like I've personally done a lot to bring plantar fasciitis to the forefront. I feel it needs to be talked about more.

I'm still dealing with it. Some days I think it's almost gone, and others, it's back with a vengeance. I have built back up to walking two or three miles continuously without any pain, as long as I walk on a smooth surface and keep a pretty steady pace. But I also know that any slight variation can cause it to flare up. I am just careful to stop walking when it starts hurting and take a break and stretch it some.

I hope this isn't with me for life. It's been almost a year now, and I'm afraid it might be. But I'm braced —and insoled—in case it hangs around.

I think Renee was right when she told me that she called plantar fasciitis the devil. It is the devil as far as I'm concerned too—*The Devil In Your Foot*. This devil in my foot doesn't wear Prada though. It wears Aetrex L400 insoles. Everywhere. Thanks to Melvin.

Oh, by the way, Melvin is off on Mondays and Wednesdays, in case you were planning to stop by. Also plan to wait a while, and check your ego at the door. Melvin does not mince words.

WHAT'S THE POINT?

When I stay home by myself for very long, I become pretty convinced that I'm nuts.

Like every time I walk by my new air fryer. I look at it, knowing full well that I will never use it. But I kept hearing everyone talk about their new air fryer and all the delicious meals they are making at home in just minutes. I felt I was really missing out.

Then I got some bonus points from Crate and Barrel, and saw a nice one there I could get basically for free. Keep in mind there are at least ten thousand things in Crate and Barrel I could have gotten for free —that I would have used and enjoyed—but I decided on a kitchen appliance. Also keep in mind that I don't cook.

What was the point of that? Lord knows I'll never use it. It sat in the box for a good six months before I finally felt guilty enough to remove it and plug it in. And, true to form, it is still brand new.

I've even asked some friends what and how they cook in their air fryers, listening intently trying to act like it's not going in one ear and flying out of the other. You'd think by now I'd learn that my kitchen is purely decorative.

What's the Point?

Fortunately, when I go outside and meet other people, I discover that they're obviously wasting time and money too. So I feel a little less nuts.

A few years ago, in the building where I live in Nashville, there were some frozen pipes in the parking garage—I think it was a sprinkler line. I wasn't surprised. The parking garage has all kinds of openings in the walls for ventilation, so it's basically the same temperature as the outside. That day I watched water spraying wildly from the burst pipes above, and a river of water flowing across the floor.

I was surprised, a month or two later to see an insulation crew working in the parking garage. What they were doing, though, made no sense. They were taking pieces of insulation and placing them on the bottom half of the pipe, and then zip-tying them into place. So basically 50 percent of the pipe was insulated.

I'd never seen anything like this insulating job, before or since. And this wasn't just here or there, like they missed a section. This is exactly how they insulated all the pipes in this large parking garage. I'm no scientist, but I feel pretty sure that only insulating the bottom half of the pipe won't stop it from freezing. Maybe they think that the bottom half is where the water is flowing, so they will just keep that area of the pipe warm. I really have no idea. But I have seen a lot of insulated pipes in my day, and I have seen a lot of people installing pipe insulation too, and they always go all the way around the pipe.

I stood there looking at this and thought, *Why even bother?*

I think the same thing every time I walk through

What's the Point?

Laguardia Airport.

To be fair, I am thrilled with the new LaGuardia Airport in New York. It is fabulous. And certainly fabulous compared to the old one. The old LaGuardia Airport was pretty horrendous, and badly in need of major updates. This rebuild has taken about a decade, but they have constructed an entire new facility in the same spot—while in continuous operation. That created some major traffic issues for a while, but those are mostly solved now.

I totally understand that logistically there had to be a lot of long—and I do mean long—concourses connecting buildings. Patrons were left to maneuver through some very long escalators and long walkways to get from their car to their gate.

And that is fine. I get it. I like walking.

But every time I am there, I'm baffled by this one thing. In the new terminal there are these extremely long walkways, hundreds of yards in length, even up to a mile of walking. I'm talking fifteen or twenty minutes of walking from the entry to the gate.

So, here I am, pulling my little carry-on bag behind me, walking briskly, thankful for the new, wide, bright, hallways and for the nice carpets and high ceilings. Then, about halfway through, I see a moving sidewalk. A moving sidewalk of maybe seventy-five feet in length.

No doubt a moving sidewalk is a great idea for people that aren't capable of walking or that need a breather. But in the middle of these extra-long corridors, giving someone seventy-five feet of relief—about the length of one aisle in a grocery store—is like giving a starving man one single bite of food. That

What's the Point?

bite might satisfy him for a moment, but it's not going to solve his problem.

So why bother? Does seventy-five feet of moving walkway make any difference at all? It just seems woefully inadequate, and more of a tripping hazard.

Maybe I'm wrong. Maybe that seventy-five feet on a conveyor belt is the only thing that enables thousands of travelers to get from point A to point B. Maybe it is life-changing for some people. It truly puzzles me.

But there are things that puzzle me everywhere.

Over by Belmont University, in Nashville, there is a retirement home in a six- or seven-story modern building. Originally, it was a nice-looking brick building. It appeared to have been built in the '70s or '80s, and there was nothing at all wrong with it. The bricks were an attractive color. It was nothing earth-shaking style-wise, but a nice-looking brick building. I could see no reason to change the exterior.

But they did.

A few years ago, they spent a lot of money and resurfaced the entire building with a bizarre combination of shiny silver panels and rusty metal panels. These weren't panels that happened to be painted a rust color, these were metal panels that were already rusty. Over the years, they have become completely covered in thick, dark, orange-red rust. I suppose this was the intended look—maybe the rust is supposed to contrast with the bright silver panels.

Oh, did I mention that the building is a senior living facility.

Seriously? Did anyone give any thought to the optics here? It's a building full of old people—

What's the Point?

covered with rusty metal panels. The symbolism is just too on-the-nose for me. I don't want to be reminded—by the building I reside in—that I'm old and aging and rusty. Or did anyone maybe just think for a moment that a building covered with rust-covered metal would be ugly?

I don't get it. Maybe the design is just too clever for me.

If I still don't feel sane after going out into the world and interacting with other people, I just go online.

Lately, on Instagram I've noticed a large number of women posting very frantic videos. They say they are going to a black-tie party or a wedding that night, and have just received a package of six or eight dresses that they ordered the day before.

Apparently, none of these gals have a calendar, or any time-management skills, because they all just remembered, or were just invited to, this major formal event and are desperate for your help. They model each dress for you, their followers, and then want you to weigh in on which dress they should wear.

Usually, none of the dresses look very good. They don't fit properly, or are just ugly to start with. The person in the video is always in a huge hurry, and begging for advice as they stretch, pull, and try to zip the dress while speaking into the camera. They stress, over and over, how little time they have, and how they need you to weigh in immediately and give them advice.

It's similar to the people flipping houses on HGTV where everything has to be done by tomorrow. If they finish the home just one day late, they will miss the open house, not make a profit, and never sell the house—basically the world will end. They are frantic. I had to quit watching those years ago.

But these crazed women seem to pop up more and more often in my Instagram feed. No idea why. I guess because I occasionally look at the comments and they are probably tracking my activity. The followers get really invested and give real advice—as if they believe the person actually does have a real black-tie event that night.

It's all seems very fake, and a ploy to get followers and comments. But the commenters do make their opinions known, and sometimes they get into fights with other followers over their choices. Then there is always a discussion about body-shaming, and invariably weight issues come up, and everyone gets offended.

Interestingly enough, there are never any follow-up photos from these events, showing which dress they wore, and who they went to the event with, etc. Nothing. And you know good and well, if these young ladies went to a black-tie affair, they would be posting tons of photos and videos.

And yet, about a week later, this same person has another formal event, and has ordered a bunch more questionable dresses to try on—desperately begging for viewer comments.

What is the point of this? I have no idea.

I'll file this in the same folder with my questions about women who date and marry men in prison. I don't get this either. What do the women get out of this exactly? I'm sure men marry women who are in prison too, but I always hear about the women. I hear about it a lot on *Dateline* and other true crime shows, so it happens more than you think. Many of these women seem very intelligent and sane. I suppose a husband that can provide no money, no companionship, and no sex might have some perks, but what are they?

Maybe the main perk is that you always know where your husband is. Maybe the woman was cheated on in the past and wants a man that she can keep tabs on. Well, prison ought to do it.

Though I can't help but be perplexed.

I tend to look at everything logically, but something that seems logical to you might appear totally pointless to me. So, even though I want to understand your thinking, I've decided there are some things I just can't figure out and I never will. So I'm throwing in the towel.

I quit.

And really, who has time to worry about the point of things anyway? I have a new air fryer that needs dusting.

BOONETOWN SQUARE

Fifty years ago, in the early '70s, the Boonetown Square was still thriving. Encircled by busy merchants who had been there for decades, it was the place you went for anything you needed. I knew all the stores, what they carried, and who worked there. I always went shopping with my mom since I was the youngest of my siblings, and they were already in school. I loved the buzz from all the shoppers and businesspeople on the go.

Of course, this was long before Walmart existed. I think maybe the Big K had opened in town by this time, but it was way up on the main highway. At the time, no one understood that those big, new stores signaled the end of the downtown square as we knew it. The square still had a good ten or twenty years of prosperity left.

There was the First National Bank where my mom worked—before she married and for a few years after—and Brown's Department Store right next door, where I got all my extra-long jeans. I think each quadrant of the square had a different five-and-dime store. I loved to go in those. They had games and toys and cleaning supplies and home décor items.

Basically, an earlier version of the Dollar General stores we have today.

There were two or three department stores on the square. They sold men's, women's and children's clothing, as well as some home goods. My favorite among them was Parks-Belk. Belk's, as we called it, was a large store with men's and women's clothing departments, plus a good-sized home goods and fabric department in the basement. They were so well stocked with adult goods that their children's department was in a separate, smaller store close to the main one.

At the young age of eleven or twelve, I could tell that Parks-Belk had the most stylish and trendy clothing of the stores on the square, at least as far as the children's departments were concerned. They also had the best home goods. And they had my other favorite thing: a gift-wrapping service.

Back then, every store offered free gift-wrapping. Not just sticking it in a bag with a piece of tissue paper, like today, but actually placing your item — nicely folded — into a real box, wrapping it in festive Christmas paper, and adorning it with a bow. They made the bows in the store on a metal machine with a crank handle. I loved that.

At Christmas, Parks-Belk had so much demand for wrapping that they set up large tables in the basement and had three or four gift-wrappers working all day during the holiday shopping rush. Even with this staff, there were always lines, and a brief wait.

Funny, back then, you would have never considered going home without having your packages wrapped in the store. For one thing, it was a time-saver. But mainly it just somehow made the gift seem better if it had an in-store wrap job.

I loved standing there, watching the pros wrap our packages. These were usually high school junior or senior girls working part-time for some Christmas money. And I will be honest here: this would have been my dream job.

I wanted to be a package wrapper so badly. I knew I was just as good and just as fast as those girls. I also knew I was too young. I thought about it, and felt sure that when I got older, I would surely apply.

After all, I had plenty of practice. I wrapped all of my mom's packages, and of course mine, and she would take me out to my grandma's house every year at Christmas and I would wrap hers. Mom would have already taken Grandma up to Rose's Department Store where she would buy simple gifts for all her friends and farm neighbors in her small community. These were inexpensive tokens mainly—kitchen towels and potholders, bottles of lotion, and things like that.

Grandma would give me each gift and watch in amazement as I folded, boxed, and wrapped them. I'd always create a fun bow for each package. She would always say that the wrapping job looked more expensive than the gift, and that made me work even harder on the bows.

Mom and I would always get tickled when we went shopping with her. Grandma would say she wanted to get gifts for all the "little old ladies" in Henryville. Then my mom would remind her that she was older than all of them. But Grandma never quit referring to her neighbors as little old ladies.

I never got to be a package wrapper. By the time I was old enough for that job, there was another job on the square that caught my eye. It was at Wilson's Men's Store.

Every year, Charlie, the owner, would hire a high school student for the summer and after school. Wilson's was a really nice men's store with nice suits, casual clothes, and lots of good-looking shoes. It was in a cool old building too. As I outgrew the children's department at Parks-Belk, Wilson's became my new store of choice. I wanted so much to work there. I wanted to be that year's sales assistant. I could see myself helping customers as they selected suits, shirts and ties. I felt I would be a natural at putting together interesting color combinations.

This, too, was not meant to be. Back then I thought Charlie always hired one of the popular boys in high school, and that certainly wasn't me. And I couldn't even wear most of their clothes. I was so tall and skinny that few of them fit. So, I didn't feel I would offer a fair representation of their goods. By that time, I was already working part-time at the family business, so I really wouldn't have had time either. I never applied, but I sure wanted to be the one selling those clothes.

The square also had other shoe stores, some nice women's clothing stores, a couple of furniture and appliance stores, and a couple of drug stores. I loved to go in the furniture stores, but mom seldom let me in one of those. I was always trying to talk her into some new furnishings for our house. That was not high on her list of priorities.

When I was in the eighth grade, I discovered a new shop. It wasn't technically on the square—it was just a block behind the Parks-Belk store—but it was very close. It was in a large, old, red-brick, Victorian home. Not a mansion, but pretty close. Boonetown was a farming community and wasn't blessed with much great architecture, but this house boasted so many nice details. I went in the shop with some friends to buy my eighth-grade teacher a gift, since we were graduating. We ended up buying some nice candles...but I ended up starstruck by this house.

It had everything: high ceilings, beautiful woodwork, multiple fireplaces, huge windows, a magnificent staircase. It even had a turret too. What more could you want? I studied it intently before we left, wanting to stay longer. My friends didn't understand my fascination, but I was in love with this house.

I was thirteen at the time, so it wasn't like I could buy it, and it wasn't even for sale. Still, I went home and immediately drew up plans. I remembered that the downstairs had oddly shaped rooms with lots of angled walls and little vestibules. But we hadn't been able to go upstairs or into the back part of the house. Still, I knew I was pretty good at drawing floor plans from just looking at the exterior of a home, so I rode my bike back by the house, studying the locations of the windows. After I drew the plans as best I could, I did what I still do to this very day. I drew in all the furnishings in the various rooms. Lastly, I made a mental picture of what each room would look like under my design guidance. I loved the mental images I created.

I would stop in there occasionally during my high

school and college years, on the pretense of shopping, but really to study the house. At some point, the store closed, and the house began a long decline into disrepair. This was much like what was happening store-by-store and building-by-building on the square. When Parks-Belk moved to the new shopping center near Walmart, I think that was the final blow for the downtown.

After I graduated from college, I was asked to join the Main Street program in Boonetown, and I was happy to do so. Main Street had been very effective in revitalizing many downtowns all around the country. I had seen it in action and wanted to be a part of it. But want and reality are two very different things. I think I did my part, offering free design advice to anyone who would make an investment in their property, working at fundraisers, and attending lots of meetings.

Unfortunately, there were still so many absentee and uninterested landlords, it was like beating your head against the wall. They would close their store, and then just let the building sit there and rot for years on end, never considering what that did to the overall image of the downtown. We watched it happened over and over again.

Or someone with an idea, usually underfunded and not well thought out, would rent a building—because space was very cheap downtown—and try to make a go of a new business. I told some of my friends on the Main Street board that it was hard to get excited or have confidence in a new business when their sign is written on the front window in white shoe polish. Sadly, those businesses usually lasted about as long as the shoe-polish sign.

It was so depressing. The older merchants didn't want change, didn't want to make any investment, and were opposed to most anything Main Street tried to do. And they were the very folks we were trying to help. It was an inside joke at Main Street that we would never be able to improve the downtown until some people died. As bad as that sounds, it was true. Those older landlords—that would not keep up their buildings nor let go of them—needed to die off in order to see any real progress.

I even designed and, with help from friends, built a museum in one of the public buildings on the square. We tried everything to bring people back to the square. Nothing seemed to be very effective.

In the following years, there would be spurts of investment here and there and then nothing. It was so frustrating. One year the square would appear to fill up with new business ventures, and then the next year it would look emptier than before. This went on all through the '90s and the early 2000s.

But you know what? Those disengaged landlords did die off. And buildings finally started to change hands. At last, some real investment was being made, and a lot of great old buildings were saved and updated. I didn't agree with all of it, and some of the design choices left me speechless, but most of the buildings are still in-tact and occupied. As a matter of fact, in the last few years, our little square has become much more vibrant, and is filled with cars in the evenings as people dine at some of the new restaurants.

My nephews and I even bought a couple of buildings and restored them. They have living space on the second floor, and retail at street level. My niece recently opened up a great new shop in one of our buildings, and it's a fantastic addition to the downtown. There are quite a few people living on the square now too. People are now fighting to buy buildings downtown that couldn't be given away a decade or two ago. It's far from perfect, and still has a long way to go, but it's in the best shape I've seen it in since my college days. And with that I am very pleased.

You might be wondering about the house. Every time I went downtown I feared that I would see a pile of rubble on the ground in its place. For years, buildings were being torn down all over the older parts of town, and this building was literally crumbling. But before it was hit by the wrecking ball, a couple bought it. Hallelujah.

They didn't just buy it, either. They did an excellent, thorough restoration and returned it to its former glory. All the woodwork was saved, and they brought back the true Victorian colors and décor. After they finished the restoration, they asked me to come over and consult on some exterior work. I was happy to — I wanted to see the results.

This house that I had fallen in love with was now, once again, a showplace.

And as of this writing, it's back on the market. Which kills me. Every time I drive by, I want to buy it and put my stamp on it. What fun that would be. But that's just it. I just want to redo it. I don't really want to live there. It's way too big, and I love my neighborhood too much to move. Oh, how tempted I am, though.

Maybe someone will buy it and let me do the interiors for them. That would be ideal. If you are reading this and interested, call me. I'll give you a great rate, just to get my hands on that house—that old house that feels like an old friend.

For me, some buildings really do feel like old friends. Especially structures with so much history and such distinctive architecture. It was there before I was born, and I hope it's there after I die.

Some of the buildings on the square feel that way to me too. I fondly remember shopping trips there with my mom, and the way the windows were decorated. Wilson's always had the best window displays, but Parks-Belk had great ones too. It was a close race.

Up the street from the square is the old theater where I saw movies as a kid. Coincidentally, I recently finished redesigning and reworking the backstage area of that grand old building, making it more functional for today. But it is linked to my childhood and always will be.

These days I travel a lot. I visit towns far more beautiful and grand than this place I was raised in, and where I've spent most of my life. Boonetown has changed dramatically over the years. Thankfully it is in a sort of rebirth right now.

I sure hope that continues.

Because no matter where I go, or live in the future, it will always be my hometown.

Speak Up

I think I am going to start wearing a scarf—loosely around my neck—to all future meetings. The reason? I was in a meeting the other day and I had a full-out diva moment. Tantrum. Fit. Call it whatever you like, but to me "diva moment" sounds a little more dignified than the others. And, I am just going to admit it right here, it felt damn good.

I had become very irritated—I think justifiably so—with a couple of people who had barged into a meeting I was having with one of my favorite clients.

They proceeded to push all my buttons.

Hard.

And I decided to gather myself and my samples, and leave.

So, I did.

But not before loudly proclaiming my major lack of giving-a-damn about their opinion. As I turned to storm out the door, I suddenly felt a strong urge to fling my scarf over my shoulder. Such a nice exclamation point.

The only problem was I wasn't wearing one. So the air-fling gesture that I produced only looked as if I were having some sort of involuntary spasm. But I did manage to successfully storm out the door—in a huff.

I try hard to not let things get to me. And I have become immune to a lot of irritations that used to really eat at me. Most of the time when people say things that really annoy me, I remain quiet and hope that they—not I—prove themselves to be the fool. I think it was Abe Lincoln that said, "Better to remain silent and be thought a fool than to open your mouth and remove all doubt."

So I try, I really do try, to not prove myself a total fool. And the vast majority of the time—I'd go so far as to say 90 percent of the time—I don't embarrass myself. But there are those times, those moments when, for lack of a better expression, I intentionally or unintentionally show my ass.

Those are the times when I truly believe it is heart-healthy and mentally stabilizing to just open your mouth and say what you are thinking—let it all out. There is some freedom in it, I think—sticking up for what you believe in and not getting run over.

Sometimes it's brought on by years of irritation with someone, or with something out of your control. Other times it might be the only way to get someone to shut up and listen. And then, there are times when you just want to get your way.

I was in the old Parks-Belk children's department when I had my first public hissy fit. Well, there might have been others, but this is the first one that I recall.

I acted so bad it was memorable. But it was for a good cause—a pair of purple corduroy, bell-bottom pants. I was probably eleven or twelve at the time, in the mid '70s. I'm not sure why we had stopped in the store, but we must have been there for something. My mother didn't take me into a clothing store for no reason.

I recall my mother talking to the clerk when I spotted them. They were purple with legs that flared from the knee down, sporting lavender corduroy patch pockets on the front and back. The pockets really set them off. I wanted them so bad I could taste them. I was in love. This was at the height of '70s hippie-chic-mod fashion, and these were just like the pants that all the men were wearing on my favorite TV variety shows.

My mother was not amused nor interested. But I had to take a stand. I knew if we left the store without them, she would never bring me back, and even if she did they would be gone. I asked first, giving all the reasons I needed them. She said a firm, "No." She explained that they were hideous, and that I wouldn't want to be seen wearing them. (More likely, she wouldn't want to be seen with me while I was wearing them.)

I asked again. A flat no.

Then I begged, quietly—at first.

Still no.

I got louder.

I had never been one to make a scene in public, and my mother was not one to tolerate it either. But I felt strongly that these pants were worth the risk. I think Sonny had worn a pair like them recently on the *Sonny and Cher Show*. Mother argued that no one at school would be wearing anything like these pants.

"Of course no one at school has them," I said, "that's what makes me want them so much."

The more she refused, the louder I got. It was a standoff.

There might have been crying, I can't remember for sure. But it was a very ugly scene, I am sure. I'm not proud of it, but we left the store with the pants in hand. Mom wasn't happy about me in the purple pants, but I sure was. I don't think she took me shopping for a year after that. It was worth it though.

Really, that was a pretty isolated incident. As I recall, I was a very well-behaved kid.

But as an adult, I often find myself wanting to speak up, wanting to throw a fit, or toss out just the right cutting comment at just the right moment. I usually think of the perfect thing to say about ten minutes after the conversation has ended.

I love people that speak their minds, though. People who say what they think and make no apologies. You always know where you stand.

Sometimes I want to be more like my friend Amy's mom. She would always let you know what she was thinking, even at a funeral.

We were all gathered around her husband's grave on a very hot summer day. Amy's dad had passed away during an August heatwave. Everyone was miserable and, since an eighty-year-old man was being buried, the crowd was mostly older. There was no shade, and I could feel the sun blazing down on my head and shoulders.

The preacher and family were under a tent, as they usually are, and the preacher was standing near the next of kin — Amy, her mom, and her brother and

Speak Up

sister. He spoke, and obviously knew the deceased, Amy's father, very well. He had a lot of stories to tell, but they seemed more about himself than the departed. It got hotter and hotter. I could literally feel the skin cancers developing on my head. He had gone on for about forty-five minutes. Amy's mom wasn't having it. She was squirming. I could tell she wanted to get everyone into a cool space. About that time, she looked at the preacher and said, out loud, "Ok, it's time to wrap this up."

I almost belly laughed. Without a doubt, that was one of the coolest things I'd ever heard uttered.

The preacher kind of laughed, and said he would wrap it up, but then proceeded to talk ten more minutes. He was totally oblivious to the fact that he had a group of eighty-year-olds standing around in one-hundred-degree heat, literally melting into their orthopedic shoes.

I doubt there is anyone, anywhere, who hasn't wanted to tell a preacher to "wrap it up" at one time or another. Everyone has wanted to, but never had the guts. Amy's mom was a trail-blazer. No doubt about it.

I can't say I was surprised though, because I had known her daughter Amy for close to twenty years. Amy doesn't hold back either. I think she got it from her mom.

The first time we met, I was at a gathering and I heard her in the other room speaking loudly. I didn't know this yet, but Amy often speaks loudly, and so I tuned in. She said, "I don't want anyone standing around my casket saying that Amy had the neatest kitchen, the cleanest bathroom grout, and a spotless house. I want them to say that Amy was a great friend, fun at parties, and good in bed."

I realized right then that Amy was someone I wanted to know. I immediately assessed myself, and remembered that I had been home, that very day, scrubbing my grout, instead of being outside enjoying the day with friends. She was my new role model.

Her Facebook posts are some of the funniest things I've ever read. She has no pretense and suffers no fools.

I remember another time when I was hired to do a design job at a large bank. They had me do a lot of work there at the main office, and also at some of the branches. It almost didn't turn out that way though. If one of the employees had gotten her way, nothing I proposed would have been done.

It was in the initial meeting that things kind of went sideways. I was making a presentation for the first phase of work at the bank. The group that was assembled were the folks I expected. I had met them all, and I knew their positions in the decision-making chain. One lady, though, was unexpected at the meeting. I had no idea who she was. I figured she must be pretty important, because I had only been dealing with the top folks.

I had put together a scheme for a large reception room—a room that is, to this day, one of my favorites I've ever done. All in shades of blue with lots of varied textures in the upholstery fabrics, and with English antiques, black leather chairs and beautiful art. It was pretty gorgeous I must say. So I was confident. I could see the finished product in my head, but I still always worry that the clients won't be able to see my vision.

Things were going well, until the unknown woman began interjecting every few minutes. She started off every question like this: "I watch a lot of HGTV, and on HGTV they..." or, "On HGTV, they are using a lot of..."

I was getting more and more irritated. The things she was bringing up were things she had seen done in homes, not a public space. It felt very much like an attempt to fluster me. The other attendees seemed to be frustrated as well, but I still wasn't sure if she had any actual authority. I hated to make her mad if she was a decision-maker.

The longer things went on, I began to notice some real irritation on the faces of the other bankers. I felt that I needed to shut her down, or I would never get this meeting wrapped up. She continued though, and said, "Well, on HGTV they aren't using wallpaper anymore."

I said, "Yes, but in commercial buildings wallpaper is still used often."

Then she said, "You know, I was watching HGTV recently and they aren't using blue right now."

To which I replied, "Yes, and they are promoting current trends while I am giving you a timeless look."

The final straw came when she again said, "I watch a lot of HGTV and they said—"

I interrupted her mid-sentence, "Well, you know, I watch a lot of the Surgery Channel, but I don't hear anyone paging me to the O.R. to consult on brain surgery."

No response from the lady. A few suppressed

giggles from the others.

For once, I thought of the right thing to say, and said it at exactly the right moment—it served its purpose well.

Funny thing, after the meeting I found out that this woman wasn't even invited to attend the meeting. She just joined in because she felt she had valuable input. Everyone there thought someone else had invited her, so no one questioned her presence until after it was over.

I'm not sure what happened to her but she wasn't at any future meetings. I guess she was busy watching HGTV.

So I say this: if the situation warrants, speak up and speak out.

Take a stand, demand to be heard, stick up for yourself, say whatever you feel necessary. Sure, you might end up humiliated or embarrassed, but you might end up feeling refreshed and vindicated.

Just let me add one piece of advice. Try to stop a sentence or two before you think you are done. I have found it's always those last couple of lines, that hold the most hard-to-take-back verbiage. And remember, the less often you have a big moment, the more shock-value it has, and the more seriously you are taken when you do speak out.

Whatever the case, if you feel you are on the verge of speaking up, acting out, or having a hissy fit, you might want to wear a scarf.

A PARADE PASSES BY

It's graduation season at Vanderbilt. The chairs are out. I love it when they put the chairs out. Vanderbilt has an outdoor graduation ceremony and they place hundreds—actually thousands—of white folding chairs, in perfectly spaced rows, all over every inch of the great lawn in the center of campus.

A temporary stage is assembled at the lower end of the lawn since the chairs cover every other available inch. I first noticed them around twenty-five years ago, when I started staying in Nashville on the weekends and would walk around the campus for exercise. I look for them every year.

I love all of the tradition in this setup. The chairs were there, on that same great lawn, when my sister graduated from Vanderbilt back in the '80s. It's pretty much unchanged.

I don't think I noticed it then, but these days I do notice that the workers place strings on the ground, pulling them very tight, to create guidelines for the chairs. I love to see the symmetry of it all when they first place them. The perfect spacing and the precise layout connect with the perfectionist in me on a very deep level.

It's a lot of work and a lot of preparation, but for what you pay to attend Vanderbilt, I think you should get a little pomp, symmetry, and ceremony on the way out the door.

After the ceremonies are over, the perfection is just a memory and the chairs are a scattered mess. But they aren't that way long. The crews arrive the next day and start removing them. That's quite an operation in itself, and it's just as interesting to watch.

One thing that has changed at Vanderbilt during the twenty-five years I've been in Nashville is the dormitory move-in process. I don't know exactly when the change started, and I am sure it has changed gradually over the years, but it has definitely changed.

I remember helping my sister move into her dorm room at Vanderbilt. It was a pretty basic process. My parents and I pulled the family car up to the nearest available parking spot and got out and carried all her stuff—ourselves—to her room. My sister had driven her own car with the rest of her stuff—which we also helped unload. It took a few trips, but was done in short order. I think we went to lunch at the Cooker or somewhere nearby afterward. This seemed to work just fine.

So I was quite surprised, recently, when I was out walking on Vanderbilt "move-in" day. Things had changed dramatically. First of all, there was the parade.

All the parents and students had pulled their vehicles into an assigned parking lot, and they were directed into lanes. Then, after receiving a signal from the dorm, the police—sirens blaring and lights flashing—escorted the parent's vehicles, parade-style,

A Parade Passes By

from the parking lot around the corner, down the street, and into the dorm parking lot. The only thing missing was a marching band. I am sure that by now this omission has been rectified. I do, of course, appreciate that things run more smoothly when well organized, but, I'm sorry, the police sirens blaring just seemed a bit much to me.

But that wasn't all.

When the parade reached the dorm parking lot, there were dozens of upper-class students, all in matching t-shirts, waiting there, cheering and waving welcome signs. Dance music was blaring out of portable speakers, with balloons and refreshments all nearby. As the cars and SUV's parked, another group of students in the same matching t-shirts came flooding from out of nowhere with hotel-style luggage carts.

They literally attacked each vehicle, opened the doors and hatches, grabbed all the student's bags and boxes, placed them on the luggage carts and ran— that's right, I said *ran*—with them back to the dorm. I have no doubt they also unloaded the cart's contents in the dorm room. The parents and the student just walked behind them, with maybe a bag or two.

As this was happening, the other students were still there, cheering, high-fiving, and yelling out greetings to the new students.

Granted, it is an accomplishment to get into an Ivy League school like Vanderbilt. But seriously? I would think carrying in your own stuff isn't too much to ask. Personally, I would prefer to carry my own things. But this is a different generation and a different time for sure.

A Parade Passes By

I had to stop my walk and watch—in utter amazement—as this process unfolded. At one point, I had a flashback to my move-in day experience at UNA and burst out laughing right there on the sidewalk. It would have been hard for the two experiences to be more different.

It was 1980, and I since I knew I would be sharing a dorm room, and knew I wouldn't have a lot of space, I packed pretty light. My mom kept offering to go with me, but I saw no need to ruin her day. After all, I had my Chevrolet Chevette hatchback, so I could carry everything I needed. I think she finally did insist on coming along, just to see what my dorm room looked like. I hated to depress her like that, because it was quite retched, but almost all dorm rooms looked like that back then.

When I got there, I simply parked in the parking lot. Inside the lobby I found a bored-looking upperclassman sitting at a table giving out room keys. No cheering, no balloons, and no music in the background. I don't remember anyone even offering a warm welcome. There definitely was no parade.

There were a few old grocery carts you could use to load your stuff in and move up to your room. I'm pretty sure these were found in the dumpster at the nearby Kroger since none of them had four operating wheels. So the carts didn't prove to be much help. But I had packed lightly, so once I got my 1,000-pound mini-fridge up to the room I was pretty much finished.

As I said, this was a different time.

We all had the same J. C. Penney ripcord bedspreads, except in different colors, and not much else. No one in my dorm had upholstered headboards or matching linens, and I didn't see any well-coordinated room décor either. This is something that has evolved over the years, too. Dorm room décor has definitely improved.

But the kids I was watching move in at Vandy were not only having a different move-in experience, I knew they also had an entirely different high school, and overall growing-up experience than I did. Their lives have been so much different than kids of my generation. I have no doubt their college experience will prove to be much more enjoyable than mine too, especially considering they started day one with a freaking parade.

As I thought about all this, I knew that the very last thing I would have wanted when I moved to the dorm would have been that type of reception. I'm not really into a lot of fanfare. I felt that carrying my own stuff to my dorm room was appropriate. It would have been nice if they had some better carts, with operating wheels, but a low-key move-in suited me just fine.

So, I stood there, watching this move-in parade with one realization. Kids are now celebrated and they have options. All kinds of options. And the parents are there for it.

Take, for example...Travel Ball.

Growing up, it seemed like we were inundated with sporting opportunities. But I hated sports and wasn't one of the athletic kids. Seeing kids play every sport imaginable only made me feel more awkward and geeky. But apparently, there weren't enough opportunities with school-affiliated baseball and basketball and football and soccer and softball, or community and Little League t-ball, soccer, and so on.

Now, we now need to pack-up our families every weekend, and travel to other states to play ball. Why? I have no idea. I suppose they are all having fun. And I guess they are getting in lots of ball-playing experience in their pre-teens and teens. Or maybe they are just getting completely burnt out on sports by the time they apply for college. Oops, did I let that slip?

Travel ball didn't exist—that I knew of—back in the '70s, but I feel one hundred percent sure that, even if it had, and even if I had wanted to participate, my parents would have never gone along with it.

Back in my youth, you couldn't record, stream, or re-watch anything that came on television or the radio. Every family had a set regimen of TV shows that they watched every night, after the evening news, of course. It was a pretty rigid schedule around my house and most of my friends' homes as well.

There had to be something huge going on in order for my dad to miss *Bonanza* or *Lawrence Welk*. Dad never allowed any of us to use the remote control either. He was in control of programming. And if you weren't there, in front of your TV on that Saturday night at 8 p.m. to watch your favorite TV show, you missed it.

Forever.

Sure, there might have been one re-run in the summer. But that might or might not occur. There were no guarantees. You had one shot each week to see your favorite shows, and it was do-or-die. If you missed them, you were out of the loop the next day at school, or had nothing to talk about with your coworkers at the water cooler.

Then there was Dad's Saturday afternoon standing golf game. That was sacred. It was not missed. Ever! Except for sleet or ice storms.

So, the idea that my dad would pack up our family every weekend and head out to some barren ball field and watch me play ball was laughable. I will say that if I had played Little League ball—which, thank God, my parents did not force me to play—and if my team did make some kind of finals in a tournament in another city, Dad might have missed one game of golf or one episode of *Lawrence Welk* to come watch.

Maybe.

But every weekend? No way.

My mother always said that if her funeral ever fell on a Saturday during his regularly scheduled golf game, to just ask the hearse to loop by the country club so Dad could pay his final respects.

Now, however, with streaming and working online and all the benefits of the internet, parents no longer have an excuse to stay home. They are more mobile than ever. This, to me, is just one more way in which today's technology has double-crossed the adults.

So they pack up the families and head out to whatever small town is hosting that week's tournament. Places that seem rather primitive to me. Not a Broadway touring company in sight in these little weekend stop-overs. Just dusty ballfields and maybe a McDonald's. But the parents do it. And the crazy thing is, they seem to enjoy it.

Personally, I can't think of anything much worse.

Somewhere along the way, it seems to me, that the kids got possession of the family remote control. Then they got their own TV and a game console in their bedroom. Then they were never heard from again—until time to play ball or eat.

Eating has changed drastically too. Now, it seems kids get to choose what they eat. I don't have children, and I am sure I would probably do the same thing if I had kids, but every time I hear parents having a discussion with their children about what they would like for dinner, I want to horselaugh.

In all of my childhood, I cannot ever, not even once, remember being asked what I might like to eat for lunch or dinner. Mom came up with the menu, bought the groceries, cooked it and it was delicious. If you didn't like something, you had the option not to eat it, but there was no other choice waiting in the refrigerator. It was always good though, and I can't remember ever not wanting to eat it.

I do recall that on my birthday Mom would ask me what kind of cake I would like—I always wanted German Chocolate—but that was pretty much the extent of my decision-making.

Everything has changed for us all over the years, even the way we communicate. Having a regular conversation seems to be passé. Now it's a stream of text messages with so many emojis splattered throughout that I need a translator.

I try.

I really do try to embrace them—these hellish little symbols—but they are so small I can hardly decipher what they are, even with brand new glasses. When I finally focus in on what it is, then I have to try to understand the meaning. Is the emoji laughing or crying? Is a smiling rabbit emoji different from a smiling puppy emoji? Is a tilted smiley face saying something different from a straight smiley face?

Help me. Please.

Oh, and I just hate it when I send a text to someone and they just stick a heart emoji on the corner of the message. Ok, so you liked my message, but do you want to have dinner or not? Then I message back asking about the aforementioned dinner and they respond by sticking a little thumbs-up emoji on my message.

What the hell is that supposed to mean? Ok, I guess you want to go, but when? Where? What time? Type some words, for God's sake.

It also seems young people have an aversion to actually talking on the phone. I like hearing your voice. I can tell things by your inflection. We can make multiple decisions in just a few seconds about when, where, and what time to have dinner and not have to exchange a hundred texts. By the time I've worked through all the texts and symbols, I'm just irritated.

The worst thing though is when old people—like me—try to use emojis. It just never works out. We usually can't see the little things to start with and then we don't know what they mean, and this just leads to problems.

My friend Maggie was telling me about her granddaughter, and all the texts the granddaughter was getting from her other nana on the other side of the family. The young girl told Maggie, "I think Nana is losing it. She is signing all her texts to me with five little piles of poop after her name."

Maggie said, "Well, I think you should tell her. I'm sure she doesn't realize what she's doing."

Turns out Maggie was right. Nana thought she was signing her texts with little Hershey Kisses. And she was doing this with all her friends and grandkids. Instead of the kisses she thought she was sending, she was actually just sending little piles of shit.

I'm not sure if she is still using emojis or not, but I bet she is thinking twice.

By now, this group of Vanderbilt students I was observing had all their possessions carried in for them, and their parents were now pulling away to park elsewhere. I could see another parade of parents and students rounding the corner.

Personally, I've never been given a parade. But there was that one time I was *in* a parade. It was a Christmas parade, and I was in it totally by accident.

I was on my way to a Christmas party in Alabama, driving through this small town that only had one main road. I could see that there were some cars and floats and bands lined up on the streets that were perpendicular to the main road, and I figured they were getting ready for a parade, but no one re-routed me or stopped me.

As I drove further along, they stopped the traffic and let all those parade vehicles on the side street enter in front of me. In my rearview mirror, I could see them releasing all the parade vehicles onto the road from the side street I had just passed. Suddenly, and against my will, I was right in the middle of a Christmas parade.

I had no decorations, no candy, no sign—nothing. I could see the puzzled look on everyone's face, as they tried to figure out who I was and why I was in the parade. The kids along the route looked especially irritated. A couple of them even knocked on my car window wanting candy. The other vehicles had passengers tossing out treats. I had none. I've never disappointed so many people in one afternoon. (Except maybe my high school coaches.) I tried to look straight ahead, but I could still see the looks of confusion.

It was the same look I was giving these Vandy students on the way to their new dorm rooms. Sure I was confused by this move-in spectacle, but I had to laugh too. I realized that life—for better or worse—never stays the same. This next procession of SUV's rounding the corner and heading to the dorm was yet another parade that had passed me by.

WARDROBE DYSFUNCTION

I have the worst time with suits. They never fit right off-the-rack so I have to special order, and then I still have to make lots of alterations. Then they just hang there in my closet, taking up space until I have a wedding or a funeral to attend.

But I did have a wedding to attend. It was a fall, outdoor wedding on a beautiful piece of property my brother and I owned. My oldest nephew was getting married. I was planning to wear this sage-green suit. (I know. Green? But it was popular at the time.) I had bought it a few years before the wedding. I hadn't even worn it once, so it was basically brand new—still hanging in the garment bag it came in.

I got dressed and headed out to meet my sister. We were riding out to the wedding together. About half way there, she said, "Did you spill something on your jacket?"

I looked down at my sleeves. They weren't stained, but they were full of holes—like a piece of Swiss cheese.

Damn moths.

I suppose the suit fabric had a high wool content

because the jacket had been seriously munched on.

It had turned really cold that day, so to go without the jacket was not an option. Then I realized that going without the jacket was not an option for another reason. I had just gotten a good look at my pants. They had been feasted on too. There were holes all up and down the legs.

What size were these moths? They had to be huge because they had eaten a forty-six extra-long men's suit from top to bottom. That's a lot of fabric. I was suddenly scared to go back home and face those massive moths.

By the time we got to the wedding, it was very cold, and I was feeling very ventilated. I was praying for an early sunset and dark lighting at the reception. As it turned out, I don't think anyone really noticed. But I will say this: it was the first time I have ever come home from a wedding, taken off a brand-new suit and thrown it in the garbage.

A few years back before that, I had purchased a flax-colored linen suit from J. Crew, especially for this European tour I was going on. I wasn't performing in concert or anything—like that sounded—it was just a vacation. As usual, the sleeves weren't long enough, so I went through the long, tedious process of letting out the jacket sleeves. I learned how from my mom. I have to do that on most of the jackets I buy.

First you have to take off all the buttons, and undo the hem, add some extra lining inside and extend out the part of the hem that is turned-up in the sleeve. After that you have to sew it all back in place, by hand, and then sew all the buttons back on the sleeve.

It takes a few hours, and I do believe the expression pain-in-the-ass was invented just to describe this painstaking project.

But I got it done, then I packed up and headed off on this ten-day adventure. When I arrived and unpacked, I realized that the small bottle of shampoo I had packed—inside of two, tightly zipped, Ziplock bags—had leaked all over most of my clothes. The hardest hit was the suit jacket.

I immediately put everything in the bathtub, and figured it would just need to be rinsed out and dried. How much harm could some shampoo do? It's just soap.

But the minute that jacket hit the water, it was as if a red-dye bomb hit. The water covering the right side of the jacket turned red, and I was intensely aggravated. Where in the world was this red color coming from?

I looked all over it. There was nothing red anywhere on the jacket. Then I checked the front pocket and found this small piece of paper with "inspected by Sharon L." printed on it in red. By this time the letters "Sharon L." had run down the paper. So I knew it was all Sharon's fault.

Believe it or not, that little bit of red ink had turned the water red, and my flax jacket shades of pink and red. I rinsed and rinsed and finally got the damage down to one large pinkish-red spot on the front pocket of my jacket. I had invested a lot of time in that jacket and I was really mad.

I was planning to wear that suit several times over the course of that trip. And once again, I had been betrayed by my wardrobe. Every time I wore the jacket, I had to hold my arm just right over the stain, or hide it with a theater program. Sometimes, I just carried my jacket over my arm. I worked it out but, damn, I was pissed off at Sharon L. the entire trip.

But at least I did get my order from J. Crew. I can't say the same for Maggie and Talbots. Just a few months ago, she was shopping on the Talbots site. She was eyeing a purple coat-and-sweater combo. So she went back to view it a couple more times.

A couple of days later, at about two in the morning, Maggie was unable to sleep and started browsing messages on her phone. As luck would have it, there was a message from Talbots, and that very coat and sweater was on sale. Not just any sale, but 90 percent off.

She felt like it was too good to be true, but she couldn't pass up a beautiful Talbots coat for $14.00 and a sweater for $9.00. So she placed the order. The next day she told me about it, and how she felt like Big Brother was watching her online search history. The more she thought about it, the more it seemed too good to be true. I agreed.

A few days passsed, and the items had not arrived. So, I suggested she check the tracking. When she read the tracking history out loud, we both burst into laughter.

It said:

Shipment arrive 11/14/23 dock Shanghai, China

Unload crate 11/16/23 dock

Move to barge transport Sri Lanka, leaving two weeks

Update when barge unload port.

All our questions were answered. I said, "I wouldn't count on the coat for this winter, maybe next."

Maggie told me another story about one of her coworkers, and it just really sums up what I have always known: no matter how many wardrobe issues I have had in my life, women, without a doubt, have it so much worse.

Ladies have so many more garments and under garments and accessories that can create problems. We men have no room to complain. And then of course all the pressure on women to look thin in their clothes only leads to more trouble.

I hate it when my clothes are tight. And my clothes are never skin tight. I remember my mom wearing a girdle and talking about how miserable it was. Now we have Spanx. There isn't much difference between Spanx and a girdle as far as I can tell, they both look quite torturous.

Maggie was at her co-worker's grandmother's funeral one warm spring day. Carrie, the coworker, and her grandmother had been very close and she was visibly upset. As the family was processing out of the chapel, Carrie saw Maggie standing at the end of a pew and leaned in for a hug. Maggie had noticed Carrie crying as she was leaving and thought she needed some emotional support. She might have, but that's not what the hug was for.

As she hugged Maggie, Carrie whispered, "Go to the bathroom and get my Spanx out from under the vanity. I couldn't stand the pain, but I paid too much to leave them behind."

Maggie understood completely and rescued the

Wardrobe Dysfunction

hidden Spanx before heading to the cemetery, offering the kind of support Carrie really needed, as only a good friend can.

These wardrobe problems pale in comparison to my friend Ellen's though. Back in the '90s, at the Boonetown Country Club, Ellen was having a great time at the New Year's Eve Dance. She was on a first date with this new guy she was very interested in, and she was wearing a brand-new jumpsuit. Jumpsuits were the hot thing at the time. Ellen loved the way her new jumpsuit looked because it elongated her petite frame. The only downfall—as any woman who has ever worn a jumpsuit knows—was going to the bathroom. She hated having to go because you practically had to take the whole thing off in order to actually use the bathroom.

But Ellen did find herself needing to go—to the bathroom—and so she did. She unzipped the jumpsuit, trying to maneuver the top in one hand as she lowered the pants portion. But luck wasn't on her side that night. The top part of the jumpsuit fell right in the commode. By the time she could get turned around to grab it, the top was already really wet and, thus, created a big problem.

First, she tried wringing out the wet part. That got rid of a lot of the water, but it was still really damp.

She tried wringing it out again, but once she got re-dressed, she was still damp from the waist up. She left the stall and bent over under the hand dryer, aiming her wet back at the air vent until she heard voices and retreated back to the stall. By now she was nervously wondering if her date had noticed how long she was gone. She couldn't go back out to the dance floor though—not wet.

It was not an optimal situation—running out and standing under the hand dryer in between ladies coming and going—and it was taking quite a while. Finally, after a lot of frustrating time under the hand dryer, she rejoined her date.

But, as I said, luck was not on her side that night. He insisted on dancing. At first, she thought this was a good idea. Thinking that moving around on the dance floor, to some upbeat music, might help dry her top. The next dance however, was a slow one, and as luck would have it, her date wanted to hold her close.

She kept trying to push him away but I guess he thought she was playing hard to get and he wanted to get closer. Ellen hoped he would think that the dancing was making her sweat, not that she was literally doused with toilet water.

She thought about making a dash for the door, hoping to catch a ride home with someone—anyone—but looking out the window she could see it was snowing heavily now, and she didn't want to be wandering around the parking lot damp and cold. It was a long, long night.

Clothes are a funny thing. If everything is going well, and you like the outfit you are wearing, it can elevate your mood, make you walk tall, and even give you more confidence.

But things can change in an instant. The garment that was once your friend can just as easily send your evening right down the toilet.

An Old Office, An Old Friend

My dad's office was always a mess and he was not concerned about it in the least. His desk was a disaster. It looked like an avalanche of papers landed there. He said he knew where everything was. He didn't.

But this office was the place he worked and the place he had fun. He did his estimates there, on the little spot he had cleared off in the middle of the desk. He also did most all of his business dealings there, at his desk on the phone, just like everyone else.

Back then, in the '70s, a group of my dad's close friends began coming by in the afternoons after work for a drink or two, before heading home. It was something that just developed over the years. That core group would end up meeting every weekday afternoon and every Saturday morning for at least thirty years — the rest of my dad's life.

This was a group of drinkers. In those days the drink of choice was Very Old Barton and, to be perfectly honest, they all drank too much of it. It was fairly cheap and they mixed it with some ice and a splash of water. They always drank from red Solo cups — there was nothing fancy about this group.

There were discussions about work and about various things going on in town. Usually an argument would break out. It was almost always something totally trivial, but these men took it personally when something happened in town that they knew nothing about, like the sale of a large piece of real estate.

I'd hear Dad yelling at one of his buddies, "I know good and damn well Walmart bought that land for a new building and I'm going to prove it."

Then Big-A would say something like, "Yeah, you stubborn know-it-all-jackass, no one can tell you anything. I heard today from John Gibson that McDonald's bought it."

Then Dad would tell him, "Just be quiet you big son-of-a-bitch, I'll find out, and prove I'm right."

By this time, Bill would have made his way to the phone, called one of his other buddies who worked at the court house, and had gotten the pertinent info needed to solve the argument. He would grin and withhold it for a while, making them both squirm before reporting to the group who had been proven right. They'd all have a big laugh about who was wrong or right, exchange a few more insults and have one last drink for the road. Everyone always went home in a good mood—no hurt feelings.

Bill was the quiet one in the group, The Researcher, I called him. Big-A was my dad's long-time best friend who ran the bowling alley, and also had a septic tank cleaning business. He was always there in the afternoon for a drink, unless he was called away for an emergency septic tank overflow. He was the sweetest one of the group, I always thought. Bill was a later arrival, joining in the early '80s.

An Old Office, An Old Friend

Bill's dad ran the bus station where my dad and his buddies had coffee every morning before work. When Bill returned to Boonetown from a stint in the navy and law school, he started hanging out there with my dad and his friends for morning coffee. Then he started stopping by our office in the afternoon.

I would see Bill there occasionally on a Friday afternoon, or a Saturday morning when I was catching up on some bookkeeping work while home from college. I'd poke my head in Dad's office to say hi. Bill never had much to say to me, and I was pretty sure he didn't like me. But I thought he was kind of cool precisely because he didn't talk a lot. There was some mystery about him.

I later realized that, even though Bill was quiet, he was always plotting and planning when he might insert a well-placed snide remark into the conversation. The more Bill drank, the more likely he would throw out one of those remarks, and the sharper they would get. He could be totally inappropriate and, if you didn't know Bill well, you might think he was an unfriendly smart-ass.

By the time I graduated from UNA a few years later, Bill was stopping by most every day for drinks with my dad and his gang. There were many others that would stop by the office from time to time. Dad's friend Ray, who was a manager at a local manufacturing plant, was a semi-regular. He traveled a lot for work so he wasn't there every day, but he was there most. Don Jackson, stopped in occasionally, as well as a couple lawyer friends of Dad's.

A man named Hal was also a regular in the '80s. He would come over at odd times—in his bathrobe—

to read the Wall Street Journal. Dad had a subscription to the Journal, mainly to track his stocks. Hal didn't. Hal also didn't have a driver's license, so he would walk from his house, a couple blocks away, wearing just his bathrobe, underwear, and slippers. He was retired and enjoyed a drink now and then, too, so I guess it made sense to him to just proceed through our back parking lot, through our shop, and head right into Dad's office.

He was so quiet, I often didn't know he was there. That is until I went in the office to put something on Dad's desk. I'd find Hal sitting there in a chair, reading the paper. With the newspaper open, and Hal's legs crossed, at first glance, it appeared as if a naked man was there, reading the Wall Street Journal —as if that were totally normal.

Dad never said a word though, and always was friendly to Hal. In Dad's world, a buddy was a buddy, no matter what—even if he was trying to conduct business with Hal still sitting there. Hal would eventually leave, but not before getting some very strange looks from visiting salesmen.

After college, I was trying to update our primitive bookkeeping system and had begun installing computers and such. The guys in Dad's office would always listen to my daily recaps as I was leaving for the day. I was excited about all the new things our computer system could do, and wanted to share what I was learning. I never got the idea they were very interested though, and Bill would just stare at me until I quit talking.

But, as time passed, once in a while Bill would stop by my office and talk with me before he headed back for drinks with the other guys. He'd occasionally look at some of the drawings I had done. But he didn't say much about them, so I never knew what he thought.

I had often mentioned my love of design. He also had heard me talk about a house or two I had been redesigning for some of my first clients. This was in the earliest days of my design career. Back then, I only worked with clients on Saturdays since I was full time at the construction business. I had lots of good ideas, but not much confidence. I guess the main reason Bill and I did get along was that Bill was not a talker and I was the opposite.

But apparently, he had been paying attention to what I was saying and doing.

One day, out of the blue, he asked me to design a river cabin for him on some property he had purchased. I knew that he had been in the **navy** before law school and that he was still in the navy reserve. He loved boating and wanted to be on the water.

I was shocked when he asked me to do the job, but excited at the same time. As I began doing sketches for him—staying true to his personality—he never showed any excitement about my ideas. But he did end up choosing one of my designs and he built the house. By the end of the project, I felt like we were on friendly terms, and I was beginning to like him, even though we had nothing in common. I just had to get used to his quiet style.

A year or two later, he suggested to his friend Sarah, that she hire me to help redecorate her home. So I met Sarah, we hit it off, and it was the beginning

An Old Office, An Old Friend

of many design jobs for her and her family. It was also the beginning a long, long friendship with Sarah.

While quietly going about his business, Bill put some things in motion that changed my life, without me even realizing the impact. He helped get my design career going. As time passed, we eased into a good friendship, and he would stop by my office for a chat every day before heading back to my dad's office for drinks with the gang.

I never got the impression Bill had a very loving family life. I knew both of his parents and they weren't what I'd call warm-and-fuzzy. They were both businesspeople, kind of gruff and no-nonsense.

His mother Reba, owned a high-end clothing boutique in Boonetown, and she oversaw daily operations from an elevated perch in the center of the large store. She liked to call the shots from her little booth, and let the salesclerks handle the one-to-one interactions with the customers. I knew this because I would go in there from time to time with my mother when she needed a new outfit, but my mother always felt uncomfortable in that store. She knew Reba socially but never felt at ease with her.

My favorite thing ever to happen in any Boonetown retail shop happened in Reba's store one day. I've asked my friend Brenda to retell it so many times over the years that I feel like I was there.

It was after Christmas, and Brenda wanted to exchange a pair of earrings she had been given by one of her friends. I guess all the clerks were busy, so Reba had to wait on Brenda herself. Brenda quickly got the feeling that Reba was a little peeved that she was returning the earrings, but Reba told her to find

An Old Office, An Old Friend

something else and she would make the exchange. Brenda looked the store over and didn't see anything else she liked and decided to just get a couple of pairs of panties.

Keep in mind that these were the panties of the '70s. They were full-size panties, not skimpy ones or thongs. They had a considerable amount of fabric. So Brenda put her little bitty box that the earrings had come in on the counter along with the panties, and she asked for the exchange. Brenda once again sensed Reba's extreme irritation at the entire situation. Reba grabbed the little box and the panties. She then turned her back to Brenda, and began to do ...something. Brenda could see Reba's arms moving and some amount of effort being exerted, but she had no idea what was going on. That is until Reba turned back around, threw the tiny earring box back on the counter and said, "There's your panties."

Brenda could hardly believe her eyes or ears, but took the box, put it in her purse and left. She couldn't believe she had been treated this way over a simple exchange, and she couldn't believe those two pair of panties were in that little box. When she got to the car, she opened the tiny box and the panties exploded out of it. Brenda burst out laughing, and then spent a good twenty minutes trying to stuff the panties back into that box.

She never could.

I've always told Brenda that I thought this was because of the lack of rage on her part. You see, Reba had plenty of rage when she stuffed them in there, and Brenda didn't. That was the difference.

Once I heard that story—and experienced Reba

myself when in the store—I had a different perspective on Bill. I think Bill felt like a part of our family and, unless his court case ran late, he was there shortly after 4 p.m. every day.

Over the years, I did many more design projects for Bill. Sarah and I would often laugh about his horrible taste and bite our tongues when we would hear that he had picked out something himself. Bill and I became more and more blunt with each other, and I think he loved it when one of his purchases threw a kink into my design.

One day Bill told me that he and Sarah were going to get married the next morning, at his home. Low key, just like the two of them. Sarah's husband had died of cancer before I met her, and she was left to raise three teenage daughters. Sometime along the way, she and Bill began dating. When they got married, Bill became a family man overnight with three adult daughters. I think that made him really happy.

We considered Bill a part of our family too: expected every day and well-known to all the office employees. One day he came in for his usual drink—it was Crown Royal by this time, they were all making more money now—but I noticed he looked bad. He looked really pale and not well at all. When he went back to my dad's office for their usual drinks, I followed him in and asked Dad what he thought—he agreed. So I called my sister.

She was a nurse-anesthetist. Luckily, she answered the phone. Usually at this time she would still be at work, but this particular day a number of things went in Bill's favor. She asked him if he felt cold and clammy, and he said he did. She asked a couple more things that I can't recall, but then she told me, "Put him in the car and go straight to the emergency room, don't even wait for an ambulance." My sister knew we were only a few blocks from the hospital and that time was of the essence. She felt sure he was having a heart attack. He was.

There was no one else in the emergency room that day when Dad and Bill and I arrived—another stroke of luck—and a nurse met us at the car. She took one look at him and took him straight back to a room.

Within minutes Dad and I heard codes being called and observed doors flying open as carts of equipment rapidly pushed through, all followed by a flurry of activity. The doctor later said he had coded as soon as he got there but was revived. Shortly after that he was air-lifted to Nashville. The next day he had open-heart surgery and four bypasses. He was indeed lucky then: he survived that heart attack.

Sadly, about twenty years later, he had another heart attack and didn't survive. He died at home in bed, peacefully and quietly, just like he would have wanted it. A memorial service was held.

It had never really occurred to me until that service—hearing speakers and friends tell stories—just how many young people he had influenced and nurtured. He did it so quietly, never bragging, never self-servingly, but with real concern and real help.

He obviously had a strong influence on his stepdaughters, both before and after he and Sarah married. And he was delighted to be a grandfather when grandchildren began to arrive. I also knew that he—quietly—personally financed my niece's church youth ministry and was a great supporter of hers. My friend Teri reminded me about all of the time Bill spent helping her after her father died. Especially when she was in college, Bill would help her do research for papers, call to check on her, and was always there for her. A young lawyer that Bill had mentored spoke about how much Bill had taught him about criminal law, and how much Bill had impacted his life.

The most touching comments, though, were provided by a young man that Bill may have influenced the most.

The young man was a grade-school student of Sarah's. She had taught him when he was very young. Sarah knew his home situation was terrible. Actually, he really didn't have a home. His parents weren't around, and his other relatives couldn't take care of him either. Sarah stepped in and did all she could and, when she married Bill, they made the decision to move the boy in.

A teenager by now, this was the first stable home-life the boy had known. Bill and Sarah supported him all through the rest of high school, and Bill sent him to college. He eventually earned his master's degree, and he is now a teacher, coach, and father.

Typically, Bill did his part quietly. I think he wanted you to succeed on your own terms, however that needed to happen. Dealing with young people is a touchy thing, and Bill understood that young people usually won't take advice, so he didn't offer a lot. But he did try to help you find the tools. Just like introducing me to a great client and friend, both of which I needed at the time.

An Old Office, An Old Friend

I spent so much time with Bill over the years, at my office and Dad's office, when Bill would make his daily stop. He never changed—always the quiet one, just listening, waiting for the right moment to make a sharp comment. He was there until the bitter end of the afternoon group. After my dad's death, and as Big-A's health prevented him from coming by, the daily visits pretty much stopped. Bill would still come by occasionally to see me and my nephews, but things had changed too much.

Looking back, I think Bill was probably one of the most misunderstood people I have known. It's only in retrospect that I realize many of the things he did for others. And that's pretty cool. Bill didn't need recognition or praise for what he did. The things he did, he did for the right reasons. He was content to stay in the background and be quiet.

After my dad died in 2006, my brother moved in to his office, that office with so much history. Then, about fifteen years later, my brother died unexpectedly at sixty-three. Once again the office was vacant.

I distinctly remember, a while after my brother's death, meeting my nephews in the hall one day, and all of us sort of looking at my dad and brother's office door.

I said, "You don't think I'm moving in that office, do you? Evers men only leave there in a hearse."

I was the next in line, age-wise, but I preferred to not be the next one to die.

My nephews both looked back at me and said in unison, "Well, I'm not moving in there either." I sure couldn't blame them.

So, it was left vacant for a year or so. Then we decided to remodel and, since we needed a bigger meeting room, we took part of Dad's old office and enlarged our existing conference room. As fate and legacy would have it, that room has been used for many, many meetings, but also for many gatherings of friends and family, as well as Christmas parties, birthday parties, and even some readings of my other books.

And I can't help but think that would make the old gang very happy indeed.

'TWAS AN EVERS FAMILY CHRISTMAS

Another family Christmas is in the books and it occurred to me that we might never be the subject of any Norman Rockwell paintings. If you are looking for warm and fuzzy, *Lifetime*-movie-style stories with group hugs, mistletoe kisses, and hot cocoa by the roaring fire, you need to look elsewhere.

This is not my family.

I accepted early on in life that our Christmas holidays were not like the Christmases I had seen on television and in the movies.

On the off chance you are ever invited to attend a Christmas celebration—or any celebration really—with the Evers family, I think you need to be prepared.

First of all, we do not, and surely would never, break out into song around the tree. A few times, back in the '70's, I can remember us singing some carols when my sister played the piano in the living room, but those sing-a-longs were pretty rare. And even though my parents had a good stash of Christmas albums—the classics like Bing Crosby and Perry Como—they were seldom, if ever, played. Certainly not at key moments like when we were opening gifts on Christmas morning.

You will not see gleeful partiers or sentimental people reading "...'twas the night before Christmas..." by candle light.

Nor will you see tears or crying: not while unwrapping gifts, not while decorating the tree, not while gathered at the dining table.

There will most definitely not be hand-holding, hugging, or people in matching Christmas pajamas.

And, on Christmas day, you'll never see holiday sweaters, games of dirty Santa, or any other such obvious displays of typical holiday jolliness.

It won't happen. It never has. It never will.

We weren't bred that way and we simply aren't capable of it.

When my oldest nephew married his wife, Tracy, she made a valiant attempt to soften us up and bring out some of our deeper emotions, especially during those most sentimental of holidays. She even tried to turn us into huggers. I would say she made some slight inroads, but certainly no notable changes. This is a tough group and we are all set in our ways. Now I'm afraid that we have become too much of an influence on her. I feel we may have broken her cheerful holiday spirit.

Here, however, are some things you *will* see at an Evers family Christmas.

You will notice, and even perhaps be amazed at, our streamlined Christmas Eve celebration. We are of hard-working, German, get-the-job-done stock: we are nothing if not efficient. When it's time to open packages, only my eleven-year-old great-niece seems enthusiastic. I fear she is becoming less and less excited as each year passes. But she's in a room full of stoic adults, so it's hard to blame her.

My dad was so "not excited" by Christmas presents that he would not even get up from his chair in the den and walk into the living room to receive his presents. This greatly irritated my mom and the rest of us, especially when we were young.

After everyone had opened most of their presents, someone would end up taking dad's presents to him — still sitting in his recliner watching golf — where he would say, "I told y'all not to get me anything," followed by, "I don't need a damn thing." Then, after a good deal of coaxing, he would cut open the end of the box with his pocket knife, peep inside, and say, "Oh, it's a shirt."

You could tell that he loved each gift and was deeply touched as he dropped them — still mostly unopened — into a pile on the floor by his recliner. Then he would order you out of the way since you were blocking the TV. He was not about to miss his golf match.

It was not all that surprising though. I can remember visiting my dad's parents and my dad's dad would always get up and go sit in the living room — by himself — when we came to visit.

Dad got it honest.

So then, it was no real surprise that my brother carried on the tradition of remaining in another room — by himself — throughout much of the Christmas festivities. He would come in the room for a short time and open a few gifts, but it was clear he was not interested. It definitely seemed to run in the family.

This last Christmas, I sat back and watched in amazement the speed and efficiency at which our family could knock out a Christmas celebration. One of my nieces began distributing the packages as the rest of us began opening the gifts. As each gift was opened, a quick photo was taken—usually by me—of the person smiling with said gift, and then the gift was placed into that person's stack.

By the time the first few packages had been opened, one of my nephews has gotten out the garbage bags and has begun grabbing up the wrapping paper and stuffing it into the bag—sometimes before it even hits the floor.

Don't even try to recycle any ribbons here. They disappear into the garbage bags swiftly along with the wrapping and tissue paper. It usually takes my young niece the longest to open her packages because she has the most and there are more photos needed. But even she, at her young age, has learned to open, assess, and move on the next package quickly.

I have no idea where we are going or why we are in such a hurry, but we are. Things move quickly and if you go the bathroom during the gift opening, you can miss a lot. Within what seems like less than twenty minutes, everyone has opened their packages, placed them all in their "take home bag" and placed it near the door. Every trace of wrapping paper, ribbon, and glitter is bagged and stuffed into the garbage can in the garage. Except for the tree, there isn't much evidence that anything has happened.

If there is an area where we might excel during the Holidays, it is in the kitchen. Everyone in my family—except me—is a good cook. So I am very thankful for that. We always have lots of delicious of food. I would say that our dining process is more in line with other families. We certainly don't linger, but we do take more time at the dining table than we take opening presents.

I think that's why we do better at Thanksgiving. On that holiday, the entire focus is on food and that tends to work better for our family. Or the Fourth of July, when a big cookout and some fireworks is all you need. These are definitely more our speed.

I always wonder how many families actually are sitting around the tree, in Christmas pj's, singing carols and sipping eggnog. I'm sure it does happen. I guess it happens a lot. But I also like to think there are a lot of families that are a bit more on the efficient side, like us.

We do take the opportunity to share some family stories of Christmases past.

My favorite was the time that the phone rang right as we were getting home from midnight mass. I think I was about six years old. It was about 1:30 a.m. on Christmas morning, and this woman called and asked my dad to come fix her heat. She told him she knew he was awake because she had just seen him at church.

This wasn't one of Dad's favorite people to start with. She and her husband had moved to town from up north when the big bicycle plant came to Boonetown. Dad always said she had a major attitude about Southerners and felt she was too good to live in the South.

Keep in mind that I'd seen Dad leave home many times at night or on a weekend to fix someone's heat.

But this time he did not. He said, "Mrs. Donovan, I know that Terry Hill installed your unit, so I'm not going to come fix it. Why don't you give him a call?"

She replied, "I know Terry Hill installed it, but he's not Catholic and I didn't want to wake him up."

We never found out if Terry Hill was called or if he came out at two in the morning to fix Mrs. Donovan's heat, but we kind of like to imagine her at home—cold—that Christmas morning.

So, it seems highly doubtful we're going to be depicted in any *Lifetime* Christmas movies. And really, when I think about it, that's just fine with me.

At least we all get along, no fights break out, and no one has ever left hungry.

How much more holiday joy could you want?

I'M AFRAID

I have a good view of the Vanderbilt Daycare Center playground. I just look out the back windows of my place. It's a much nicer playground than I ever was exposed to as a child. The kids go out every day, which surprises me in this helicopter-parenting world we currently reside in. But they go out on the coldest days and on snowy days and on extremely hot days. They play with abandon and are pretty rambunctious.

Watching them this morning, I couldn't help but notice them coming down the slide, one after another, in all different positions. They would fling themselves down head-first, or feet-first, or on their stomach, or on their back—obviously trying anything they could think of, and imitating anyone they thought was having more fun than they were. They looked so carefree, so uninhibited, and so far from afraid. It isn't a long slide, so I doubt they are in a lot of danger. Still, sliding down headfirst onto a bed of gravel could hurt pretty badly if you landed on your face.

These two-to-five-year-old kids are fearless. They operate at full speed with reckless freedom. They haven't yet learned to be afraid of falling, or of getting hit with a face full of gravel. If the daycare workers tell them to be careful, the kids ignore them.

I know nothing about child development. Really, nothing. But I do know something about fear. I think it's learned behavior. I think we are taught to be afraid. I believe we are conditioned to fear anything different, or new, or intimidating. I was encouraged by my parents, my teachers, the television—and by society at large—to be careful, to play it safe, to always proceed with caution.

Good advice for walking through a minefield, but I'm not so sure about its value for living life. Playing it safe is highly overrated.

Fear, I think, is the main thing that stands between you and all the things you want to accomplish in life. Fear can shut down a dream faster than a loud alarm clock.

At home, at school, well, really everywhere, I vividly remember being constantly reminded of the dangers of virtually everything. There was always a negative consequence to anything positive.

By the time I was a certain age, somewhere early in grade school, I needed no one to remind me of the possible negative outcomes. I could now think of all of those on my own. I had been programmed to be scared of anything new.

I remember when I went on a class trip with my fellow eighth grade graduates. We went ice skating. None of us, that I knew of, had ever gone ice skating before, and none of us had had any lessons. No one gave us any instructions that day either. The results might have been a lot different had we been given a few simple instructions, but I kind of doubt it.

By the end of an hour in ice skates, I was still

I'm Afraid

holding tight to the rail, trying to keep my balance. I would let go and try to glide, but I just ended up taking steps on the ice, not really skating at all. Being 6'5" tall probably didn't help with the balance thing, so I was struggling to stay upright.

When I looked around, a couple of my classmates —the ones I thought were more athletic—were already skating around the ice, nowhere near the rails. Looking back now, I don't think it was that they were more athletic than I was. I think the main difference between them and me was simple. They weren't afraid.

I was. I was afraid of falling and breaking a leg or an arm or something else.

I had learned that fear.

My mom was very cautious by nature, and so were most of my adult relatives. Dad was a little less worried about trying new things, but he wasn't exactly a free spirit either. So neither of them instilled a sense of fearlessness in us kids.

Or maybe the root of the problem was the nuns and teachers at school who basically poo-poo-ed anything that sounded fun. I can't say for sure. I just know I wanted so badly to abandon the security of that rail and go sailing across the ice. But I couldn't let go of it, or of my fear.

There are so many times, looking back, where I can see how fear had a direct impact on my life and the direction it took.

Not that I have deep regrets. I don't dwell on it a lot. But I know that I might be in a different place had I not chosen the safer route.

When I was a senior in high school, I was

planning to go to architecture school and had already been accepted at two different ones. I had been drawing house plans since I was ten years old. I loved design. But the more I thought about it, and the more I read about the requirements, the reality of it all hit. I was afraid of several things, the main one being all the math involved. I hated trigonometry and was struggling with it. I knew the math in college would only get harder.

I also feared going to school so far away from home, the difficulty of passing state boards, and, in general, just not being good enough. That fear of failure set me on another path.

It all worked out in the long run, but I am not an architect. I went to a different college and got a business degree. Would I have spent my life designing great buildings, had I not been afraid? I'll never know.

Some people live life with a kind of bravery that amazes me.

Like Carol Burnett. I love her.

In a way, I think of her like a family member that I don't get to see very often. Her variety show on Saturday nights during my high school years was a bright spot during a really dark time. High school for me was, without question, the most difficult time in my life. Seeing Carol Burnett—an adult—act silly and sing and dance with her group of friends made me happy. She made me believe that some adults did have fun, and did get to make a living doing something they obviously loved. No one I knew did that. Everyone in my world worked at factories, or at other jobs that were just *work*: not fun, and not very fulfilling.

Over the years, I've seen Carol on many shows and in many interviews. Just like most of the people that I really look up to, Carol did not have it easy. Her family life was troubled and she was raised just above the poverty line. But she was blessed with talent.

I've heard her tell stories of her journey so many times over the years, and I've read them in her books. She had two very lucky breaks in her young adulthood.

First of all, someone gave her the tuition money to go to college, where she discovered the joy of making an audience laugh. Secondly, a man saw her in a show in California, and offered to loan her the money to go to New York and try to make it on Broadway. This complete stranger believed that strongly in her.

So, she headed to New York City. As the story goes, someone she knew at UCLA said they had a friend, Eddie Foy Jr., who was currently in a Broadway show, and that he was a really nice guy. The friend suggested Carol look him up when she got to New York. They thought for sure Eddie would help Carol out.

Sometime after Carol got settled in New York, she remembered what her friend had said. She decided to go see Eddie Foy, Jr. that very night. She put on her raincoat and headed out—rain was a lucky omen for Carol.

She went to the stage door, asked to see Eddie and somehow got backstage to meet him. Here's the great part. He asked her, "What can you do? Can you sing or dance? Maybe we can get you an audition for the chorus."

She said, "Well, I have a pretty good voice, and I'm loud, but I'm not a trained singer and I can't read music, and I've only had one dance lesson, so I'm not a trained dancer by any means. I'm sorry," she said, "I don't think I'm good enough for the chorus."

"Well, then," he said, "what kind of job do you want?"

"I'll need to be in a featured role," she said.

That's what I call being fearless. She had the courage to ask for what she wanted. Turns out Mr. Foy was indeed a nice guy, just like the friend said. And he did give her a call, just like he said he would. The rest is history.

I finished Barbra Streisand's autobiography not too long ago. It was a fascinating in-depth look at her career and life. The way she kept laser-focused on her vision for each project—and always stayed true to that vision—was truly impressive. It's especially amazing that a woman in Hollywood during those years was able to maintain so much control over her career.

I first heard her singing "The Way We Were" in 1973. I was only eleven, but I knew even then that it was one of the all-time great songs and vocals. I've been listening to her ever since. Reading her book answered so many questions about all the phases of her career and why she did this or that. She said she never remembered a time when she did not want to be an actress and knew that she simply had to be one. There was no choice.

When she was young, her mother told her she wasn't pretty enough to be an actress in film, and said

Barbra should go to secretarial school and learn to type. Barbra defiantly grew her fingernails out longer so she couldn't type, even if she wanted to. She had no plans to be a secretary. She already knew, as a young person, that everything she did must somehow propel her toward a career in film. Singing was nothing she ever planned to do, but she did it in order to make a living while she pursued acting. It wasn't a bad fall-back career for her, since she is now considered one of the greatest vocalists of all time.

Early in their careers, both Carol and Barbra seemed to move forward without fear. Or at least they weren't scared to try.

They went after their dreams without hesitation or a back-up plan. Of course, they are both mega-talents. But had they not been fearless, that talent may have never been exposed to the world.

I have read so many biographies of my favorite actors and singers. And, like Barbra and Carol, a majority of these stars came from very humble or poor backgrounds. It seems that having-nothing-to-lose is a common thread among those brave young talents. They wanted to escape poverty, do something big. It was do-or-die for them.

And so they did.

It seems to me that job security and a comfortable home life, are huge deterrents to risk-taking and achieving your dreams. Suddenly you have something to lose, a lifestyle that could be gone if you risk it, a home that could be lost, and on and on.

I always wish I had been more fearless when I was young. I wish I had taken more chances before I got comfortable, before I settled into a life. As they say, I wish I had known then what I know now.

It takes so long to figure it all out though, doesn't it?

Luckily things don't scare me nearly as much as they used to. These days, I feel more comfortable in my own skin. And more willing to give this or that a try.

Publishing a book scared the hell out of me, but at sixty, I thought, well, what's the worst thing that could happen? So I gave it a try, and I am glad I did.

I guess there is something about aging to be happy with after all: letting go of some of the fear.

Finding that child in me that isn't afraid to go down the slide headfirst.

Having the courage to let go of the rail and glide across the ice.

Finally finding the guts to be fearless—well, at least every once in a while.

YOU KNOW

It was just a random Thursday night in Boonetown. I was out with the girls at a local steakhouse. It's one of our finer dining establishments. This is the restaurant that's attached to the bowling alley—my friends and I only eat at the best places.

We were celebrating two of my friends' birthdays. These ladies have all been friends of mine for at least thirty years. I've called them my Harlettes for years. I got the idea because Bette Midler used to call her backup singers the Harlettes and, since these ladies always have my back and have helped me out with many of my decorating projects, I felt it fit.

In our group of four, one is divorced, I am single, and the other two have been in years-long marriages.

A lot of things had changed in the last few months before this evening. My two married friends had been through a lot. Shockingly and suddenly, both of their husbands died, within weeks of each other—heart attacks we think. So, it's been a time of major adjustments.

But here we are, and we are still laughing and talking a lot as usual. That never changes, no matter what is happening. The youngest of them has just turned seventy-five and I really cannot believe it. I just turned sixty, so I am a good bit younger, but I have never viewed these women as older than myself. They certainly don't act it.

There are tell-tale signs, though, that we are all getting older. I've noticed it more and more recently, during our time together.

During every conversation, we start to play the "you-know" game. ("You-know" is what I call it. You may refer to it differently. But I bet if you are older than sixty yourself, you will get what I'm talking about.) It's a memory game. Well, really it's a loss-of-memory game. It begins with one of us trying to tell a story. Here is an example.

While we were having dinner, a lady approached our table, looking directly at Brenda. I could see that Brenda was panicked. I could tell she had absolutely no idea who this person was. Of course, as it always happens, this lady called Brenda by name and wanted to know all about her children and family.

Brenda was calm, cool, and collected.

She answered all her questions and politely asked the mystery lady about her family in return. Brenda was very convincing, and we were all beginning to think that she did actually know who this lady was. But when the woman left, we began the you-know game.

Brenda said, "I am so embarrassed, who was that?"

To which Sarah replied, "You-know, she's the woman who has the grandson that was in that bad car wreck."

You Know

Then Maggie chimed in, "Yes, he's in rehab now, but he is coming home soon. Poor thing has two broken arms. It's all on Facebook."

Brenda says, "Oh, I heard about that, but what is her name?"

Maggie says, "I wish I could think of it, you-know, her husband worked at Kroger all those years and her daughter moved to Nashville with that guy that wants to be a country music singer."

"Oh," Brenda says, "is he the one that used to coach softball? I think my girls played on his team one summer."

"No," Sarah says, "that's his brother. You-know, his brother is the one who had colon cancer last year and they didn't think he was going to make it."

"Oh, that's right," Brenda says.

"Yeah," Maggie says, "you-know his wife has the most amazing singing voice. I've heard her at church and she's right up there with Adele."

"Well, did he make it?" I say.

"Make what?" Sarah says.

"Make it through the colon cancer?" I reply.

Maggie says, "I guess so. I saw him out at church not long ago, but he looked bad. You-know his wife worked with that girl that embezzled all that money from the bank. Did she get out of jail yet?"

"Who's wife?" Sarah says.

"You know, the one we were just talking about." Maggie says.

"Wait a minute," I say, "who is the woman that came over to the table?"

Sarah says, "I thought we just told you."

"Well, I never got a name," I say.

To which Sarah responds, "You-know her name, I promise you do. I do too, and it'll come to me in a minute."

By this time, we have been down so many paths and crossed over so many family-tree branches that I have no idea who we are talking about and neither does anyone at the table. We might circle back around at some point, but it's just as likely that we won't. And that's ok, too. Because in the long run, it really doesn't even matter.

The only real rule for playing the you-know game is this: after you say you-know once, if it doesn't jar the other person's memory, you say it again, but louder, YOU-KNOW. Somehow the increased volume helps to unlock the memory.

We continue chatting and then Sarah's daughter happens into the restaurant with a group of friends, and she stops by our table. She wanted to show us a copy of the new trailer for the reality television show that her daughter, Briana, is on. It is something like *The Bachelor* series, but this incarnation is called *Farmer Wants a Wife*, or something equally silly. Fortunately Sarah and her daughter have calmed down a bit about the whole thing. You have to know Sarah to really get this, but trust me when I say, she is the very last person on earth who would want her granddaughter on any reality TV show, much less a dating show.

Sarah neither watches these shows nor finds any value in them. So of course, as fate would have it, her granddaughter Briana was chosen to participate.

Sarah had told us about the TV show and swore us to secrecy many months ago, but she had convinced us that it would never come to fruition. Sarah said there was no way they would choose Briana, hoping to convince herself and the universe it would not happen. But every time I talked to Sarah, Briana had advanced to the next step in the process.

We were all a bit concerned about how the show would turn out. We had many discussions about how, during the editing process, they could make cast-members appear however they wanted, no matter how you really acted. We were concerned that, since Briana is very quiet, they might portray her as bitchy or mean.

The next thing we knew, Briana was deep into filming, and called home to tell the family that they would be filming a home-visit right here in Boonetown. Sarah was beyond horrified. Briana's mother was as well. No one in Sarah's family wanted to be filmed for the home-visit. Sarah's husband literally had a heart attack and died the week before filming just to get out of it.

But family is family, and of course Sarah would always support her granddaughter, so she reluctantly agreed to have the home-visit filmed at her house. But Sarah also told Briana that if she showed up on TV, walking down a hallway to some fantasy suite, wearing lingerie, carrying a glass of champagne, she would be disowned by the family—forever.

I was summoned to be at the house on the day of filming to lend moral support and was pretty pleased when I met the production team. This was no two-bit operation. A couple dozen crew members arrived.

You Know

They were nothing but professional and all extremely nice. I really wanted to hang out with them a lot longer. They spent the day filming a casual lunch scene of Briana and the farmer with some family and friends. Then they videoed some quality-time footage, featuring only the young couple.

By this time, we knew that Briana was down to the final two contestants with her particular farmer. Sarah was gracious—as she always is—to the farmer when he arrived. He, too, could not have been nicer. But when I asked Sarah what she thought of him, she took me aside and said, "Well, he might appear normal, but you know there is something seriously wrong with any man who would go on a TV show looking for a wife."

I suggested she not share that with him since he might end up being her future grandson-in-law.

Late in the day, I felt I should leave because all of the crew was packing up and about to head out. I thought they needed some family alone-time with the farmer. The next morning, I called to check-in and asked Sarah how things went that evening. She said everything had gone fine and that the farmer had stayed a couple more hours after I left.

I needed more information than that. "But how did things end with the farmer?"

"Well," she said, "I told him that it was nice to have met him and I wished him all the best."

Sarah was surprised when he responded that he hoped to be seeing more of her in the future. She said, "Oh, I didn't think I'd ever be seeing you again after today, at least I hoped not."

I think that last "hoped not" was wishful thinking

on her part that just sort of slipped out. Sarah said he looked very shocked. "He was acting as if I really wanted him to marry my granddaughter."

Anyway, we all watched the trailer and it was very well done. Briana was featured in it more than once. I don't know if she was the final one chosen, but she certainly seemed to be getting a lot of screen time.

We got back to our normal conversation and the you-know game.

Brenda expressed that she was quite worried that she had been more forgetful than ever and worried she might have Alzheimer's.

Maggie said that she was worried about that as well. She had just been to the doctor for her yearly checkup. Since she had turned seventy-five, the nurse practitioner said that Medicare required a competency test to determine if she was exhibiting any early signs of Alzheimer's.

As if this weren't bad enough in private, the nurse practitioner then brought in three student nurses to observe her being tested. She said the nurse first gave her five words to remember and then told her to draw a clock face. Maggie remembered them administering tests like this to her father after his stroke. She remembered they would keep going back again and again, asking him to repeat the five words. Suddenly, she was really worried that she might fail, so she put all her focus on remembering the five words.

She knew she could easily draw a clock face. So, she thought she would just knock-out the drawing very quickly.

As she began drawing the clock, the nurse asked her to repeat the words, which she did successfully.

But then she realized that she was already up to the number ten on the clock and had put all the numbers on the right side of the circular clock face. Well, there was no covering this up she thought. "Can I start over?" she asked.

The student nurses all just looked at the floor. "I couldn't imagine what they were thinking of me," Maggie said.

I said, "They were probably thinking, she's not very smart, but she's real fast."

Maggie tried to adjust the numbers on the clock by crossing out some and moving them to the other side. Then the nurse asked her the words again, which got her even more flustered. By the time she finished, it was all a big mess. Finally, the nurse asked her to set the clock to "ten after eleven o'clock". Maggie said she thought she did that successfully.

Maggie felt sure that before she left the office there would be a tap on her shoulder and she would be escorted to the nearest memory-care facility. But as of yet, she is still a free woman. My other friends at the table vowed they would not take this test under any circumstances.

A discussion ensued about the signs and symptoms of Alzheimer's and everyone had different ideas. We all have become so forgetful with names, and that's when the you-know game begins. So, of course, this is of concern to all of us.

I told them that I had read an article recently that said forgetting someone's name or the name of an item was not really a sign of Alzheimer's. The real signs are when you pick up a fork, or something that you use every day, and have no idea what to do with it.

Whether or not this is correct, I'm not sure. But it did seem to give all of us some sense of relief. We still couldn't think of anyone's name, but we were all still able to use our utensils properly.

Brenda was on her phone checking a message as we talked about the wreck that occurred on Maggie's street. This car was parked in the wrong spot and got smashed into this ugly fence we all hate.

Then I mentioned this woman I had been dealing with at work that no one seemed to like. Everyone had a story about her and they were all unanimously bad.

Next, we were all talking about Facebook and some of the crazy postings we had seen on there. Maggie said there was a video of a guy in Boonetown that has this monkey in his house that jumps from one piece of furniture to another and all around the house. Brenda said, "Show me that monkey video. I want to see that monkey." So, we all watched the monkey video.

About this time, Brenda looked down and realized that somehow she had activated the voice-recording feature of her text messaging. Much of our conversation, in bits and pieces, had been recorded and it was still going. Finally, she got it stopped. But the message it had recorded was really too much. It was several deranged paragraphs and it went something like this.

"Use your fork, Alzheimer's, fork, utensils, yes, yes, I want a fork, use your fork, forget it, I remember my fork, crash into the fence, car crash, fence, how about a name, anybody, her, name, not her name, yes, your name, I know her name. Yeah, her, her name.

Yeah. Yeah.

Yeah, that bitch, that one, her, her, her, I can't stand, why, no, no, her, that one, with the monkey, what monkey, the flying monkey, video, video, Facebook, look at it, look, let me see, let me see it, show me that monkey ass."

We thought about messaging a few people that text just to see what they said. But, you know, you really had to be there. We were so tickled by this we could hardly talk. Tears streamed down our faces.

But this is that kind of group. We don't need a lot to make us happy. Just something simple like the image of a monkey's ass jumping around someone's living room.

The laughing must have jarred Sarah's memory because about that time she yelled out "Sally Johnson." We all looked at her with great confusion.

"Sally Johnson!" Sarah said again. "That's the name of the woman that stopped by our table earlier."

At least we got one.

I suddenly thought about being there, with those people, on a random Thursday night, in a restaurant connected to a bowling alley, in Boonetown, and realized there was no place I would rather be.

Made in the USA
Monee, IL
08 October 2024